The Revd Dr Susan Durber is minis
Reformed Church, Oxford and Cumn(
and also Joint Reformed Chaplain t(
She is about to become Principal of Westminster College, Cambridge. She was the co-editor, with Heather Walton, of *Silence in Heaven: A Book of Women's Preaching* (SCM Press, 1994) and lectures and writes regularly for the College of Preachers. Her PhD, from the University of Manchester, was on the parables of Jesus. She was a major contributor to the URC's most recent book of worship and is a member of the Faith and Order Standing Commission of the World Council of Churches. She enjoys singing, exploring historic houses and art galleries, and meeting with friends for dinner. She has a beautiful daughter, Grace.

PREACHING LIKE A WOMAN

SUSAN DURBER

First published in Great Britain in 2007

Society for Promoting Christian Knowledge
36 Causton Street
London SW1P 4ST

The publisher and author acknowledge with thanks permission to
reproduce extracts from the following:
Nicola Slee, *Praying Like a Woman*, London: SPCK, 2004.

All Scripture quotations are from the New Revised Standard Version
of the Bible, copyright © 1989 by the Division of Christian Education of the
National Council of the Churches of Christ in the USA. Used by permission.
All rights reserved.

British Library Cataloguing-in-Publication Data
A catalogue record for this book is available from the British Library

ISBN 978-0-281-05918-8

1 3 5 7 9 10 8 6 4 2

Typeset by Graphicraft Limited, Hong Kong
Printed in Great Britain by Ashford Colour Press

Produced on paper from sustainable forests

For the people of
St Columba's United Reformed Church, Oxford
'Praying to be an inclusive church'

Contents

Contents

Part 3
PREACHING THE FAITH

Preface

For more than twenty years now the rhythm of my life has been dominated by the need to have something to say for Sunday. There are times when this has seemed an almost unbearable pressure, and my sleeping hours have often been troubled by those typical preachers' nightmares about standing up with nothing to say, or finding that I am completely mute or that no one is taking any notice. But, however unfashionable or derided preaching is in some circles, I believe that this is one of the most important things I do and it remains the centre of my work as a minister, and thus of my life. This is a sacred task, to open the scriptures and to speak about them in such a way that those who listen might hear God. When I think of the awesome nature of the task, I hope I may be forgiven for suffering with what others have called, with appropriate bluntness, 'preacher's bowel'! I have long known, as I suppose all of us do, the power of words to hurt and to heal, to inspire and to move. I have known how all sorts of people, with all sorts of aims, can take words and use them to change worlds. Sometimes people criticize Christianity for being too 'wordy' and I understand something of what they mean. We need images and pictures, sounds, smells and tastes, the resonance of ritual and the evocative sounds of praise to move us closer to God. But no one should underestimate the ways in which words can be beautiful, stirring, powerful, heartbreaking or heart-mending. Words can move us to tears, stir us from our seats, rock us with laughter, move us to shame or to praise. Words can carry us to heights or knock us to the depths. Words can carry God to us and enable us to reach beyond our inner silent selves into worlds we had not imagined. Give me the right words and I can stop a man jumping to his death. Or I can persuade a woman that she is truly loved. I can persuade you of your guilt, but also lead you to the freedom of forgiveness. Give me words. As I have prepared to preach on Sundays, I have often prayed to God to give me words, give me words to open the

Bible, to speak honestly of human life and of the possibility of hope, to carry the gospel to those who listen. I am not ashamed of giving so much of my life and work to the task of finding words with which a community might name its faith or hear it expressed in such a way that strength might be found for the coming week. I am grateful for all those who have not only told me, but shown me, that this is a task worth doing and worth doing well, and that it can make a difference to individuals and to communities.

As I have learned what it means to be a minister, I have met those who have inspired me to preach, some through books and some by their presence. The American novelist and preacher, Frederich Buechner, whom I have never met though I feel I know well through his work, has taught me much about the power and wonder of language. The minister, poet and hymn writer Alan Gaunt has been a friend and mentor for many years and I owe him so much. It was Heather Walton, with whom I worked in Manchester at Luther King House, who taught me that I could find my own voice in preaching and that it could come from my own life, faith and experience. She opened for me the possibility of preaching like the woman I am, applauded my early efforts to connect my bodily, intellectual and spiritual life in what I would say from the pulpit and encouraged me to encourage others in writing this book. I am indebted to her.

I cannot reflect on women's preaching without thinking of my friend Catherine Middleton, who died aged 42 in the year 2000. She was a good theologian, teacher and preacher, and the Church lost a fine minister when she died so young. I hope this book might be a tribute to some of what she taught me and so many others.

I am grateful to friends who have taught me so much and filled my life with wonder, laughter and love. I thank Pam Anderson, a friend through many years and now a deservedly successful feminist philosopher of religion. I thank Frances Ward, a colleague from Manchester days, and so inspiring for her energy, insight and warmth. And I thank my close friend Ruth, without whose love and support life would be duty rather than delight.

Most of all, I thank the people of St Columba's Church in Oxford, who have heard more of my sermons than anyone else, with few complaints and much encouragement. Among them I have known the presence of God and the joy of ministry.

Susan Durber

Introduction

I was co-editor, with Heather Walton, of the first collection of women's preaching in Britain and Ireland, *Silence in Heaven*. That book had a missionary zeal about it and we were deeply committed to its aims. We were calling women who could seize the chance to use their voices in the pulpit to bring about change in the Church. We did not think that women would always and inevitably have an essentially different way of preaching, but we did want to argue both that women could, if they would choose to, create a new preaching language and that women would, whether they liked it not, have a different reception from male preachers given the way in which gender is under construction within both culture and Church. We neither had a romantic view of women (as naturally more experiential thinkers or as more 'earthed', for example) nor did we have a very romantic view of preaching (we were aware of its potential for authoritarianism, abuse and abstraction). But we did believe that what is said and proclaimed in church on Sunday plays an important part in the framing and reframing of the Christian faith and we wanted women to be part of that, and to be brave in using that opportunity. I hope that we demonstrated how women were already finding and developing ways to speak with voices that were self-consciously their own; speaking from the experience of a woman's body, speaking clearly of the women of the faith from the past, speaking from the Bible in ways learned from biblical criticism alert to questions of gender, speaking and writing in styles that express and even recast the faith in new ways, speaking from a Christian faith which has been both cut down and rebuilt by the critiques of feminists and womanists (theology from the perspective of African-American women). We hoped that we might encourage more women to find a new preaching voice, to question

1

the styles of Bible reading and rhetoric that they might have learned and to use the pulpit as much as any other cultural or church space to bring about the transformation of a patriarchal tradition and community. We were proud of what we achieved with that book.

Now, some years on, it is evident that there is still work to do. Even within the relatively short time since *Silence in Heaven* was published, the landscape of the Church has changed. Particularly since the ordination of women to the priesthood within the Church of England, the presence of a woman in the pulpit on a Sunday in these islands is not nearly so rare or so shocking as once it was. Though we should not make the mistake of attaching too much importance to this change in one denomination in one nation and forget that there are still major Christian communities where women are silenced, nevertheless it has been a significant cultural change. Yet, it remains true that there is, neither in the Academy nor in the Church, very much considered reflection about preaching, let alone preaching and gender. The recently published *A Reader on Preaching: Making Connections* (ed. Day, Astley and Francis, 2005) is a refreshing exception and even includes a short section on the preaching of women. But, that aside, despite the fact that preaching of some shape or other still plays an important part in almost every act of Christian worship, there is comparatively little theological reflection in evidence in the British context about its power to shape and reshape the Christian faith for our times. Among women in the Church, there is still much less said about the potential of preaching for transforming faith and worship than, for example, about prayers, art or poetry. There is some evidence that many women who preach do not enjoy it and that some of these women regard preaching as a task less appropriate or 'natural' to themselves than to their male colleagues. There are a number of reasons for these things.

In many parts of the Church there is a pervasive, even corrosive, crisis of confidence in evidence about preaching. Most books on preaching published in recent times will begin with reflection about this. We are all aware that the very word 'preaching' has negative overtones in our culture and that these have spilled over into our churches. Those in the Church, used to hearing sermons, can testify that sometimes preaching earns this negative reputation as something dull and, in its usual form, strikingly different from the much more interactive styles of most contemporary learning, let alone entertainment. There is a common suspicion that preachers 'tell other people what to think', that any preacher is above contradiction and a remnant of more authoritarian and didactic cultures which we have rightly shaken off. It is revealing that in most church communities today you can get away with making slighting jokes about sermons and preachers and there is a well-established assumption that preaching has something of the past about it. At the very least the preachers of today are asked to make use of contemporary media, like PowerPoint or film clips to redeem what they do, though even these do not answer the most trenchant (though often unarticulated) critiques of the form. Preaching often seems to stand alongside the public lecture as an outmoded form of discourse. Such a lack of confidence in preaching, twinned with reluctance in most congregations to abandon it, seems to produce the most terrible of vicious circles. In the apparent absence of imaginative forms of renewal and reinvention, many preachers seem trapped into offering sermons in a way that even they do not quite believe in any more. This, understandably enough, does not make for inspiring and transforming preaching!

In feminist circles, this general depression about and suspicion of preaching is often deepened by the belief that preaching is a particularly strong example of the forms of a patriarchal church. As Virginia Purvis-Smith has put it, 'When a clergywoman preaches from a pulpit, she enters a space which has particular aesthetic value, for this space has been occupied, and its character defined by male presence for centuries' (Purvis-Smith, 2005, p. 224). She believes that the aesthetic of preaching is at odds with the purpose of a woman preacher and quotes an example of an Episcopalian woman minister who always felt strongly that the pulpit from which she was asked to preach was 'built for a man'. In some feminist circles, preaching is thought to be something to abandon rather than to renew or reconfigure, an irresistibly patriarchal form, unfit for a new Church truly inclusive of women. In other, perhaps less radical circles of women, preaching is just little considered at all. It is thought of as one thing that the new clergywomen or laywomen do, but often not the most significant or the most loved, and certainly not particularly to be considered a place to make a difference as a woman. Nicola Slee has published a beautiful collection of writing called *Praying like a Woman* (and I am profoundly grateful for her generosity in allowing me to echo her title in my own) but there has been, until now, no equivalent book about preaching like a woman. Women in the Church have given more attention, it seems, to liturgy and prayer, to the visual arts and to creative writing than to preaching. In a book published to mark the tenth anniversary of the ordination of women to the priesthood in the Church of England (*Voices of this Calling: Experiences of the First Generation of Women Priests*) it is striking that there is so very little mention of the work, and the possibilities, of preaching. This seems all the more ironic given the title of the book! The collected testimonies of these women include many references to pastoral encounters and pastoral work, to spirituality and prayer, but very little to preaching. Lucy Winkett is a notable exception to this rule. She confesses: 'that the Church gives me authority to speak and to interpret the word of God publicly is a precious gift that I value and cherish' (in Rees (ed.), 2002, p. 198). She rejoices to 'find my place in the process where human experience interacts with the ancient wisdom of Scripture' (in Rees (ed.), 2002, p. 198). However, even she does not reflect on whether her speaking might be different or acquire a difference or even make a difference to the Church because it might be done self-consciously and deliberately from the mouth of a woman. It is interesting that the book includes some reflection from the 'old campaigners' of the Movement for the Ordination of Women, like Una Kroll. Her observation and regret is that the ordination of women has not made as much 'real change' as she had hoped and that sometimes women have acquired what she describes as male patterns and habits. Jean Mayland also argues that it is no good women being priests unless they are remodelling the Church. I have made the same observation in a book about women ministers in the Free Churches:

The true significance of the ordination of women can only by judged by its effect on the lives and spirit of *all* women. If nothing else is done, beyond ordaining some exceptional women, women in the Church and women in general may still be left struggling, oppressed and afraid. Unless we are brave enough to think more radically about gender, the fathers will still rule, gender will still be made according to unjust laws and women will still suffer violence and poverty. A much larger task awaits the daughters of dissent. (in Kaye, Lees and Thorpe, 2004, p. 214)

What may be said about ordination is just as true of the admission of women to preaching ministries (whether so-called 'lay' or ordained). It cannot be enough that women adopt the same preaching styles and take just the same texts and speak the same 'doctrines' as the men have always done (even though despite themselves they will be heard differently). If the Church is to be changed in order to become a place of true welcome, hospitality and life for women as well as men then the words with which the faith is spoken and proclaimed must be different. While preaching remains a discourse of the Church it is vital that women are speaking out from the pulpit and seizing the creative power that such a space still offers. Despite the many assaults on the sermon, it remains a place where the faith is named week by week and where it is reshaped and redefined for our times. It is the place where what might be called the 'primary theology' of the Church is spoken. Though it is under attack and, in some quarters, despised, I contend that it remains a powerful and important place for the work of theology to be done. The Christian faith is not made only in pastoral encounters and in the places where prayers are prepared and written. It is also made, and may be remade, where God's people speak of their faith, where they interpret the Bible and where they exhort the people to faith and offer hope. Women need to speak out here as any-where and not neglect the power and potential that this space may offer to them. I would argue that, instead of letting preach-ing fade from the scene or casting it off as an outdated or even irredeemable form, women could be and should be proactive in using it and reshaping it as one place where the Christian faith is being made today.

It may be the case that women have not paused to question the prevailing suspicion of preaching which often is strongest in those parts of the Church most open and welcoming to the ministry of women. For many there would seem to be an unquestionable alliance between those who regard preaching as outmoded and authoritarian, as irretrievably male, and those who are committed to an inclusive and transforming Church. If this judgement on preaching were indeed the last word it would be quite reasonable to expect that women would be less than interested in preaching. However, I believe that there are good grounds for believing that preaching can be as liberating, transforming and creative as any discourse within the Church. It does not have to conform to the models attacked by its most determined critics and has huge potential to bear truth, beauty, joy and life. Some of those who reflect on preaching today, whether men or women, bear testimony to this with great power and may provide inspiration to those who believe preaching is a tired or even oppressive form.

Within homiletics (the formal study of preaching), a much more lively subject in the United States than, for example, in Britain, debates rage about the best ways to renew preaching for the contemporary world. Some argue that contemporary thinking about preaching has been too absorbed with style and technique or even that it pays too much attention to the hearers and givers of sermons rather than to 'theological substance' (see for example William Willimon's book *Proclamation and Theology*). Tom Long has also argued that preaching has become too individualistic, or too much the community listening to itself (Long, 2004). Sermons need to convey a real sense that 'God is at work' and something new is happening. This 'school' is in part a reaction to the view of preaching established in the early part of the twentieth century by the famous and influential Harry Emerson Fosdick of the Riverside Church in New York (see Emerson Fosdick in Graves (ed.), 2004). He argued passionately then that preaching should always address problems and questions with which the people in 'the pews' were really wrestling. He believed that too many preachers were absorbed with obscure questions (like 'Whatever happened to the Jebusites?') that just meant nothing at all to their hearers. His critics argued that this approach produced sermons that were overly 'psychologizing' and which were no longer based sufficiently on the Bible (sometimes a disappointing text for addressing particular contemporary issues). The Old Testament scholar and preacher Walter Brueggemann suggests a different path through this divide by arguing that good and effective preaching is an act of 'counter-imagination'. It is 'to turn the imagination and practice of the community back to its most elemental assurances and claims' (Brueggemann, 2004, p. 13).

This seems to suggest a way that is biblical but also draws on the best insights of what some would describe as 'therapeutic personalism'. Brueggemann is convinced of the power of the preached words to address the lived world of those who hear, but also to transform it through imagination. He advocates preaching with theological power, and with real connection with the biblical texts, but his metaphors are much less of 'substance' than of 'imagination', much less of an objective 'content' than of the process of transformation.

Debates continue about the language of sermons, about the significance or not of the personality and personal life of the preacher, about forms and methods. There is a strong consensus among writers on preaching that the task of the preacher is not to be conceived as 'hunting down the meaning' or finding the one right way to understand a text. The preacher's task is not to 'tell the congregation what the text means', but to let the text speak, and it may speak in many different ways. Some writers are finding new ways of looking at the well-worn question of whether or not a preacher should speak in the first person or use stories from his or her own life. Anna Carter Florence wisely comments, 'I often wonder why we ever debate the issue of first-person stories in sermons, when we preachers don't need to say a word about ourselves for our listeners to know all about us' (Carter Florence in Day, Astley and Francis (eds), 2005, p. 105).

There is still a confidence that just as poets believe that words can change the world, so may preachers. For those who give themselves to the task of wrestling with both text and context in public, with integrity and with careful attention to those who listen, it remains true that preaching can be something transforming and life-giving. There are many writers on preaching who have the power to persuade the most timid and cynical reader that the sermon is not dead. In fact, if preaching is done with attention, passion and imagination it can provide a powerful place for the transformation of the Church, as the faith is named in words that can remake the world. No one need think that the only advocates of preaching are those who favour the old styles and the old rationales. There are plenty of those who would argue that preaching can be more like poetry than didacticism, that it can be interactive with an engaged congregation, that it can speak from and to the lived reality of human life today, that it can question and change the faith, do something other than 'tell you what to think', that it can move hearts and evoke tears and laughter on the way to truth. There are male writers on preaching who will write about the embodiment of the preacher, as the one who proclaims the incarnate Christ. There are plenty who will affirm the polyvalence of scriptural texts, the location of the sermon within the whole of the liturgy, and the sermon 'as art' whose meaning is located in style more than dogmatic assertion. There is already much to encourage a woman who thinks about being a preacher that so many of the insights held dear by radical theologians have already found their way into homiletics. It is by no means a world owned by those who want to keep the Church as it has always been. Preaching, as much as praying and pastoral care, has already found new ways of understanding the task.

But what have women to say to this? What could it mean to preach with a woman's voice? What will the insights of feminist theology bring to the task of speaking out in the pulpit? Thomas E. Troeger, a well-known teacher of preaching in the United States, argues that 'the gathering witness of women in the pulpit will disclose over time the shape of this new poetics' (Troeger in Day, Astley and Francis (eds), 2005, p. 123). It might be tempting to argue that what women bring (or have the potential to bring) to preaching is something like a new style, rather as Virginia Woolf's writing might be described as 'more feminine' without our being able to define quite what the difference is. Is it that women will be more 'personal', that they will be more 'poetic', using imagination more freely, that they will thump less and evoke more? Will they make more use of story and testimony, and less of the 'prophetic' mode? There have been those who have searched for evidence that this might be the case, though the results of such surveys have been mixed. However, what may be most important is not the question of whether women will bring their own essential or natural difference to preaching, but whether women can make a conscious choice to preach in forms, styles and words that come from their experience as women who live in patriarchal cultures and churches. Could they learn to preach from their reflection as feminist theologians who want to call for and enact change in the Church and its teaching and practice? Style is almost certainly more important than many of us suppose, for the content of any discourse changes with its form, but women preachers have opportunities to shape what the Church proclaims, believes and does as they are given voices to preach. If the Church has, at last, given some women the freedom to speak, then let us speak with our distinctive voices.

It may be true that the Church has been cautious about what women will preach and it has been careful to teach us the traditions. In a time when, in some parts of the Church, women are only just being allowed to participate fully in preaching ministries, it is natural that women themselves are sometimes cautious about doing things in new ways. We are often made aware that what we do somehow reflects upon all women! However, there are a number of ways in which women preachers can begin to preach, as a matter of deliberate choice, with their own voices and from feminist positions and perspectives. We should not underestimate the possibilities that we are given, never underestimate the women and men who wait to hear us preach the gospel and be brave in playing our part in being part of the Christian tradition in these times. There are also many in the Church who would give women preachers greater courage really to speak out and to be unafraid.

Many in Britain may be unaware, for example, of the great and strong tradition of black women preachers in the United States. In African-American churches preaching is still high-status and very much a living form. Robert Beckford reflects ruefully, in his book *Jesus is Dread*, that white Christians in Britain often love to hear a black Pentecostal choir, but never think to invite a black preacher, thus ignoring one of the real strengths of the Pentecostal churches. At the World Council of Churches' Ninth Assembly in Brazil in 2006 the only session on preaching was run by African-American Christians and included women among the speakers. There is still a high level of expectation about preaching in black churches and there is a long tradition in many of women's preaching. The women have their own traditions and voices and they are unafraid to preach as women. One collection of such sermons, *Those Preachin' Women*, begins by stating confidently that, 'it is an incontestable fact that the living Lord is choosing to lay claim upon the lives of an ever-increasing number of women and charging them to preach the gospel of Jesus Christ' (Pearson Mitchell (ed.), 1985, p. 9). The editor of this collection of black women's sermons argues that Jesus prepared women for ministry, that he welcomed women into his itinerant seminary and that it was women who first proclaimed the resurrection, so why not now? These women preach from their own experience and they are not afraid to let the Bible speak of their own lives. Again and again in black women's preaching the story of Hagar, a slave story of abuse, wilderness and the path to freedom is used to proclaim the good news of God's presence and power. Hagar speaks to them as a woman who was 'snatched from her African heritage'. In her book, *Sisters in the Wilderness: The Challenge of Womanist God-Talk*, Delores Williams also shows how African-American women have chosen not to accommodate themselves to the biblical traditions which were best known in their churches, but to accommodate their Bible reading (and their preaching) to the urgent needs of their lives. If African-American women have been doing these for decades, even centuries, then they can encourage the more timid among their white sisters to do the same.

There are also voices from Latin America that provide a powerful challenge to preachers across the world, and particularly to women. Marcella Althaus-Reid, for example, argues that much 'mainstream' theology (even liberation theology) has succumbed much too readily to the temptation to be 'respectable' and so acceptable to those in power in the Church (and in the world). She is fiercely critical of some even apparently radical theologies that, in her view, simply repeat the failures of colonial understandings of the faith. She argues that much theology that claims to speak for or from 'the poor' is built on romantic misunderstandings of poverty and that many theologians have a patriarchal and romantic idea of womanhood. She is fighting for a re-radicalization of theology and for women to find voices of their own, to come out of the silence imposed on them by a Church that has conspired to stay 'respectable'. She writes, 'Women's tongues were silenced for centuries. What survived entered into a covenant of silence, and since then it has never fully spoken again' (Althaus-Reid, 2000, p. 11). She asks why some theology pretends to be done 'with women's eyes' when the truth is that women's eyes are 'meant' to be lowered! She makes an uncompromising critique of those who suggest that women's theology can start with Marian theology, since Mary is nothing like the truly embodied women she encounters whether on the streets of Argentina or in the Edinburgh where she now lives and teaches. She rails against what she calls 'vanilla theology', a safe and unadventurous kind of feminist theology which does not want to risk disapproval, and she advocates the much more pleasurable option of an 'indecent' theology which will dare to speak from the realities of 'being a woman' in today's world. She calls feminist theologians (and by implication, I would argue, women preachers) to be much more daring in their critiques and in their writing and speaking of theology. For example, feminist theologians and preachers have sometimes taken Ruth as a biblical woman hero, but why not say boldly that it is *not* to be the Christian norm for a girl to sleep with her boss! She challenges us to be braver and to take what chances we have to speak the truth that so much 'decent' theology works hard to obscure. She writes, 'Women are the traditional consumers, not producers of theology' (Althaus-Reid, 2000, p. 170). But she encourages women to become producers. I would argue that one place to do that is in the pulpit, in the work of preaching. She recognizes in her later book, *From Feminist Theology to Indecent Theology* (2004), that women who do produce theology will always be accused of betrayal, but she is unafraid. She believes that all women's ministry is exercised in exile, because Christianity has been appropriated as a male religion. If we do not recognize this reality then we will fail to address it. Jesus asked people, 'Who do you think I am?' but now women need to ask Jesus (and his Church), 'Who do you think we are?' She calls women to move beyond involvement in what the Church deems 'women's issues' and to be heard doing basic theological things like reframing Christology and the Trinity. Again, I would argue that preaching is one place to become involved in doing just this. Where we have such opportunities we should use them. To learn to preach 'like a woman' is more than an exhortation to find some new styles, to include more personal stories or open vulnerability, to preach on the Bible stories about women or to resurrect a lost female tradition. It is to be prepared to bring into voice what has been silenced in the Church, to offer both a challenge to the patriarchal traditions in which Christianity has been embedded and a remaking of the faith in more inclusive and transforming speech. Women need to 'come out' and to find spaces where they may speak for the God who created women and men in God's image and the God who is creating a new humanity.

In *Praying like a Woman*, Nicola Slee writes, 'A woman may imbibe the sense from many quarters that she has no right to speak, no reality worth articulating, no authority to declaim – perhaps particularly in the religious realm' (Slee, 2004, p. 58). In this book of poems, prayers and reflections she advocates the finding of a new language to 'sing and stutter and shout all we've been aching to say' (Slee, 2004, p. 3). She writes to the Church, in a poem called 'Storming the silence':

> Dear brother Church,
> I am standing here as a woman struggling to be who I am.
> I am speaking;
> Are you listening?
>
> (Slee, 2004, p. 31)

If you can pray like a woman, can you not preach like one too? Is it possible that women could find, create and bravely use new languages in the pulpit, as we name and remake the faith for our own times? And isn't it possible that we can do this together, learning from one another, and supporting those who bravely take a leap away from the 'decent' theology which our fathers and brothers have taught us?

In this book I hope to encourage preachers, and especially women preachers and potential women preachers, to believe that the space of preaching is an important place for women to inhabit and to make our own. I shall offer some examples of my own preaching and with them reflection on how I produced them, how I prepared them and what I hope they might contribute to the reshaping of the faith from the lives, experience and theological reflection of women. Some are timidly 'decent' and others more daringly brave. They have all been preached before actual congregations; most of them at the two churches in Oxford where I am minister. Neither congregation would see itself, I should think, as a hotbed of radical theology, but they are both communities of Christian people doing their best to serve God in today's world. They have had a woman preacher for several years and I hope they have, at some level, noticed a difference. But they remain churches in what might be called the mainstream. Preaching and ministering in the centre of Oxford offers many temptations (as with most places) to conform, to please and to comfort. I hope that, at least sometimes, I have avoided those temptations and have been able to offer words which might recast the faith, speak from the place of a woman in culture and Church and bring good news to those God waits to set free. I hope that what I have written will encourage women to speak out and men and women to listen.

Part 1

PREACHING FROM
THE TEXT

The Bible in a woman's hands

A few years ago I wrote an article that gained me some notoriety. I remember the time when someone, having seen this article quoted in a book, said to me, 'Did you know that there is a biblical scholar with the same name as you?' At first I felt rather crestfallen that it hadn't occurred to the person concerned that the article might actually have been written by me! But thinking about it, I realized that the content of the article could well have put them off the scent. The article was called 'The Female Reader of the Parables of the Lost' (Durber, 1992) and the main thrust of it was that texts construct their own readers, that the reader of the parables in Luke 15 was definitely intended to be male and therefore that women had either to choose to read the parables as a male or not to read them at all. The article ended like this: 'Many of us have indeed succeeded in reading as men without noticing it. Alternatively, we can refuse to be constructed as male and so be excluded from reading the text. We will not find new feminist readings, but find it impossible to read these texts at all' (Durber, 1992, p. 78). One of my friends said at the time that the article was brilliant and accomplished (!), but rather sad. And I can see now, looking back, that it must have seemed unlikely that the author of such a text would turn out to be a minister of the Word, reading the Bible and preaching it week by week. So, have I decided then to read as a man, accepting that the Bible intends its readers to be male and that the only way to do it is to pretend, or allow yourself to be a transgendered reader? Was that article empty posturing? Or had I decided to live in separate worlds, being as it were a conventional minister by day and a feminist biblical scholar by night?

I think you might say that I have joined what you could call the 'resistance' when it comes to reading the Bible and preaching from it. I have not forgotten that in the world of biblical studies, feminists venture into occupied territory, and on to what seems unfriendly ground. But I am also convinced that there is an important task to do, and that if we simply 'evacuate' this work will go undone. I am grateful for the spies who have gone before me, for those who have suffered in the fight, and to those who have bravely defied the conventions to which I once felt I was completely held captive. I have discovered that, as with any revolution, there are a variety of possible tactics, and that though the situation we face is undoubtedly dangerous and fearful, there is hope and even joy to be found in the struggle to reach a new place.

First, I want to admit that it is perfectly reasonable to expect that a feminist could not bear to read the Bible, let alone preach from it. We can be almost certain that all the biblical texts were written by men and they all have an androcentric bias. The concerns of the writers are concerns derived from male experience and the presumed and ideal reader is always male. Stories and texts about women are few in number in the Bible and the women characters that there are tend to play stereotyped roles. There are some biblical texts that document appalling abuse of women and some texts that have been used, both overtly and covertly, to maintain the subjection of women. Many lectionaries have simply worked to intensify the patriarchal bias of the biblical texts. Some have sought to temper it, but so far none have overtly challenged it. Kathy Galloway, the leader of the Iona Community, tells a story about a time when she was a visiting preacher and had asked for the story of Vashti, from the beginning of the book of Esther, to be read at the service. A woman got up to read and as she began to read it became clear that she had not rehearsed, or even looked at, the reading at all and that it came as a complete shock to her. Her reading voice rose higher and higher as the scandal of this text became more and more apparent. She was clearly horrified by a profoundly sexist text and she could hardly bear to read it. And why should we have to read out, in a place we call holy, stories, injunctions and visions that seem to endorse and hallow the oppression of women, violence against women and the dehumanizing of women? I was once in a cathedral when a girls' choir was singing Evensong. The New Testament reading turned out to be a frankly misogynist passage from 1 Peter 3. The girls, who despite my hopes were actually listening, giggled. I was glad that they could laugh, but of course it isn't really funny at all. If many of the texts that ask women to be silent, that ignore us completely, or recount tales of our rape or abuse, if many of these were about black people, few would feel they could laugh. It is not funny. When we have seen how the Church has had to be dragged kicking and screaming into affirming women, celebrating their ministry and accepting that it is not childbearing which earns us our salvation, then we can see how dangerous these texts have been. We should not be deceived either by those who say that the faith communities have been at the forefront of the campaigns to bring justice to women. They have not, and they have almost always resisted them at every step. Even in my own Reformed tradition, it is only within the blinking of an eye, in terms of history, that women have been eligible to vote at church meetings, to lead the church's worship, to be teachers of theology, or to contribute towards the ways in which the faith is told.

But having said all that, I have not ceased to read the Bible, even the bits that are hard to bear. And week by week I open this book and preach sermons spun from reflection upon its pages. On the one hand, seeing what a dangerous text this has been, I am determined that women should be involved in the reading of it, and the public interpretation of it. It must be vitally important that our experience, insights and imaginations are brought to the interpretation of the Bible. Let us not leave it to the men! And let us believe that what we bring to the task of interpretation and proclamation will mean that the living text will speak anew. I do believe that this is a holy text (and in saying that I am also saying that I do not expect holy things to be 'good' in the moral sense) and that, again and again, as it is read and interpreted, God is made present. Women's preaching is by no means only about damage limitation! It is also about liberating part of the sacred potential of the text. But first, how might women preachers learn from the insights of feminist biblical studies?

Elisabeth Schüssler Fiorenza is a feminist biblical scholar who has written about the potential of the Bible to provide a liberating

19

text that works to inspire and empower women to overcome their oppressors (Schüssler Fiorenza, 1983). She sees the Bible as an ambiguous book, at once patriarchal and oppressive but also liberating. Rosemary Radford Ruether is another feminist biblical scholar who argues women should read and interpret the Bible because there are some good bits, some golden threads, and that it's worth looking for those (see, for example, Radford Ruether, 1983). The best parts of the Bible are the liberating parts and the rest of it, the oppressive parts, need to be read and judged in the light of these. Both of these women work hard to help us find the 'real' measure of the Bible; either the 'prophetic thread' which runs through it, enabling us to read it in a liberating way, or the hidden history behind it, in the light of which we see a different story. They both work hard at reconstructing early Christian history. Schüssler Fiorenza argues that all history is a selective view of the past, that the history the text silences and hides is there to be found and that this reclaimed heritage will bring power to the oppressed. So she observes, for example, that Luke/Acts makes no mention of women missionaries, but that Paul's letters disclose to us a different picture of an early Church in which women were actually apostles, missionaries and prophets (see Romans 16.1–16). She claims that there was once an authentic Christian community, a true discipleship of equals that later (though admittedly not much later) became patriarchal and exclusive of women. She encourages us to read, and also to preach from, the Bible because it is among the few precious sources we have for a history, that when it is uncovered by faithful and attentive scholars, in fact becomes profoundly liberating. By reading the Bible with an eye for the lost history behind it we can discover what she calls a 'dangerous memory'. So, what you are often really reading is not so much the text as the subtext, and it is in this subtext that freedom can be found. Both Fiorenza and Ruether provoke a kind of archaeology of the text that seeks and hopes to discover 'better news'. Their work has been very fruitful, though some have pointed out that the success of their project depends on there being a liberating hidden story or a golden thread. What if it cannot be found? Must women then remain where they have always been? There are, it has to be admitted, some biblical texts where even the doughtiest critic will find little for her comfort.

Phyllis Trible, a feminist who approaches biblical texts from a literary critical perspective, tries something else. She defends the Bible's importance for women not by saying that, despite appearances, there's much that's positive. Instead, she shows how important it is to be clear about how awful it really is, a tactic, if you like, of naming and shaming. She offers the text and its readers the possibility of confession and, thus, also forgiveness. Trible does not cover or hide, but rather puts absolutely in the foreground, the misogyny of many Bible texts. She deliberately brings to the attention of her readers stories from the Bible of appalling violence and abuse against women; like Hagar the slave (Genesis 16.1–16; 21.1–21), Tamar the princess who was raped and discarded (2 Samuel 13.1–22), the unnamed concubine who is raped, murdered and then dismembered (Judges 19.1–30), and the daughter of Jephthah, a virgin offered in a terrible bargain with God (Judges 11.29–40). She does not want to rewrite these stories to make them happier or to 'dig out' more cheerful stories that they might hide, but she hopes, in highlighting these stories which might be hidden for shame, that they might inspire repentance. She describes her project like this. 'It recounts tales of terror in memoriam to offer sympathetic readings of abused women . . . and to pray that these terrors shall not come to pass again' (Trible, 1984, p. 3). She reveals what has been hidden in the hope of bringing about repentance and change in the heart of the faith community. Perhaps we could say that she works at reading and interpreting the Bible only because she hopes to achieve something significant by being utterly honest about it, by uncovering its horror and letting it speak the truth about women's most bitter experience.

But feminist biblical scholars have found yet other ways to read the Bible. Alicia Suskin Ostriker, a poet and biblical scholar, takes up the Jewish traditional tool of midrash, and argues that all texts may be 'broken open' and read against themselves to derive blessing where there was previously no more than a curse. She goes so far as to rewrite the Bible stories so that they do offer something good for women. She even holds workshops on midrash getting women and men writing Bible stories again, using the basic building blocks and themes of the Bible texts, but turning them to a new task, telling them from the woman's point of view, in a different voice. She simply won't let the Bible alone and argues that there are loopholes and repressed meanings that can be exploited for our use. She believes that stories and texts cannot be controlled by anyone and certainly not the male elite, and she urges all readers to play freely with them! She celebrates the great potential of language to say what no one ever intended it to say and to be reused for new causes. So she boldly rewrites biblical stories to create a new women's literature. She writes,

> I will argue, as provocatively as I can, that the biblical story of monotheism and covenant is, to use the language of politics, a cover-up; that when we lift the cover we find quite another story, an obsessively told and retold story of erased female power . . . these same canonized biblical texts, and the traditions built on them, encourage and even invite transgressive as well as orthodox readings; then that the outrageous rewritings of biblical narrative by women poets, far from destroying sacred Scripture, are designed to revitalize it and make it sacred indeed to that half of the human population which has been degraded by it. (Ostriker, 1993, pp. 30–1)

While some feminist scholars work by being suspicious of the biblical texts, Ostriker works with a 'hermeneutics of desire' and encourages readers, interpreters and preachers to bend the text so that it can speak new, and use the Bible as a poem out of which one makes other poems. In a telling phrase, she writes, 'If the Bible is a flaming sword forbidding our entrance to the garden, it is also a burning bush urging us toward freedom. It is what we wrestle with all night and from which we may, if we demand it, wrest a blessing' (Ostriker, 1993, p. 86).

But Heather Walton suggests that none of these feminist approaches to reading the Bible go far enough. She argues that in the foundational stories of our faith women are marginalized and that in the present day a male guild of biblical scholars guards access to scriptural knowledge. She looks at the options women are given in reading the Bible, to read the 'good stories' and ignore the bad, to reclaim the bad stories and rewrite them, or to retell the history of the text 'in memory of her'. But all these approaches still give the ancient text the pre-eminent place. She writes, 'It's as if women were issuing a supplement to the Bible and saying to their sisters, "If you read the Bible with this in your hand, it will mitigate the text's misogyny." But the majority who read the Bible aren't protected in this way ... For the majority of women, the Bible remains a powerfully dangerous resource' (Walton, 1993). She remains uneasy, because too many feminist approaches are overly anxious to fit the living woman to the text, to stretch the Bible to fit, because (if you like) deep down we want to keep wearing it, even though we know that it doesn't fit us any more. She turns to women's writing, novels and poems for an alternative place where women's lives can find meaning and expression. She is determined to tell the stories that are not told in the Bible. Marcella Althaus-Reid is also reluctant in any way to give space to those who will minimize the challenge of reading the Bible as a feminist. She writes that 'Feminist theologies represent an authentic Christian conversion, a turning away from the structures of patriarchal sin and a reading of the Scriptures which throws the texts into crisis' (Althaus-Reid, 2004, p. 3).

As a minister within the Church I am deeply caught up in the life of a community that is both mystical body and human institution. I have long let go of any false expectations that it should be perfect or that I (of all people!) could make it so. I have decided, as if in the end I could really do anything else, to live in the real Church, with all its faults and contradictions. I have no desire to live in a ghetto, whether for safety or for exclusion. I would rather brave the cruel world. I have to admit that the Bible, in many of its parts, is indeed deeply ignorant of women's lives and often cruel in what it says. Those who make clear to us the patriarchal bias of the biblical writings, and of the straightforward misogyny of some particular texts, are absolutely right to do so, and their challenge should not be underestimated. But in some places, in the cracks and fissures of this text, I find a space still to be, whether to fight and resist or to receive grace beyond dreams. I value the sense the Bible gives of connection with the communities of the past. I want to travel into that space even if there is much that will be strange and frightening and much that I do not want to bring home with me. It will not be the only place I will ever visit and I will not dwell always and every minute only there, but I cannot resist regular invitations. I also no longer believe, as once I did, that texts are entirely in charge of their own interpretation or reception or determined by the original intention of their authors. The biblical texts, as many have noticed, are very spare, and leave plenty of space for readers to find a way in or a place to wander. And I no longer feel that to be a good reader I have to be a compliant or passive one. I am ready to fight with the text and argue, as once I argued with my father and with male ministers and priests. I have enough cheek to think that if the Bible is still to be read in the holy places then there must be some here who will speak for the women whose voices are so easily excluded or silenced or ignored. So, I am committed to reading the texts of the Bible, week by week, and to working to interpret them for the community of faith. I am also glad to find that there are many tools for reading them and for finding ways, learned from feminist biblical scholars, as from others, to let them speak anew. I am shamelessly ready to use whatever ways I can find of letting these texts speak and of praying that God will speak as I work and labour upon them.

The sermons that follow in this section make use of various methods of reading that one might call feminist. They are ways that this particular woman has found to read and to preach 'like a woman'. They are not all the same. They are not necessarily consistent. But they are all self-conscious attempts to preach the gospel from a feminist standpoint, making use of tools devised by others, to find something interesting, arresting and in some sense 'true' to say from the pulpit.

The sermon on the Gentile woman who argued with Jesus (Mark 7.24–30) and the sermon about the women at the empty tomb at the end of Mark's Gospel (Mark 16.1–8) both make use of historical feminist approaches, of the sort pioneered by Elisabeth Schüssler Fiorenza. The first story, a text that does emerge with regularity through the usual patterns of the lection-ary, is rather a gift to a feminist preacher for the way it represents a moment when the scandal of the gospel breaks through the natural attempts of the early Church to make things tidy. It's amazing that it made it into the tradition at all, but wonderful that it has. Here is a story of a woman pushing Jesus' theology further and persuading him to heal a Gentile, not a Jew. It's a story that becomes even more astonishingly liberating the more you find out about the broader historical context. While it does not take much to see that this text has huge potential for affirming the power and daring of women who challenge male assumptions, a feminist reading can take it further by comparing it with other stories in the same Gospel about daughters and their parents. Then the significance of the story is more powerfully revealed.

The sermon on the empty tomb addresses a perennial textual puzzle about the end of Mark's Gospel, but does so through feminist historical studies. While it is textually puzzling that the women should have remained silent, it's not a surprise from the point of view of the feminist historian. An article by the feminist biblical critic Mary Cotes inspired this sermon (Cotes, 1992). But a sermon is not, of course, anything like the same thing as a learned article. In the sermon, the insights of history are connected with wider women's experience of being silenced or of falling silent, and the resurrection is imaged and the coming to voice and speech at last of what had been kept quiet.

Several of the other sermons in this section reflect something of Phyllis Trible's approach, of telling Bible stories about women in order to name real suffering and to address it. The story of Jephthah's unnamed daughter (Judges 11.29–40) does not make it into the lectionary. Stories like this one have to be deliberately chosen. I was inspired to preach on it after I had been to hear Handel's oratorio *Jephthah*. The programme notes were wonderful, explaining the ambiguity of the end of the story, the terror of this tale and its place in a culture struggling to know how to treat its children. As the audience spilled out of the theatre, I could hear them discussing the story and their reactions to it. I remember thinking at the time that preaching should do just this for those who listen, by provoking such a deep and emotionally charged engagement with the text that people are transformed, moved and challenged. This is a text of terror, but it can also be a liberating and transforming story. As I preached from it at the baptismal service for a girl, I sensed that the Bible is a text which, because it names what we dare not name, addresses subjects and themes from which we must not turn. It was not hard at all to let this story speak, as it had done so powerfully from the stage of our local theatre.

The story of Salome (Mark 6.17–29) is another kind of 'text of terror'. In this case (curiously enough, another baptism sermon), I engaged not only with the text itself, but also with the history of the text's interpretation and reception. It's striking that many of the biblical stories about women have a particularly rich interpretive history. They've been painted, filmed, made into musicals, plays and operas, and served as the focus of academic study. They provide ready material particularly for the visual arts, since, as we know, women have always been the subject of the 'male gaze'. In the sermon I deliberately compared what had happened to this text with what might, or might not, happen to a woman's life and offered a more hopeful possibility and challenge. The sermon makes use of contemporary history, of a lively re-telling of the story and of reflection on the text's own story. This is a text that the lectionary uses, but in this sermon I have told it as Salome's story, not as John the Baptist's. He has his day on other occasions. This technique, of reading a text from a different place, noticing an apparently marginal character, can provide a new entrance to the story and stir new ways of seeing and understanding it.

The sermon on the story of Mary and Martha (Luke 10.38–42) also looks at the history of the text's reception and pulls the hearer towards a fresh hearing of the text by reviving a sense of its context (in a tradition in which stories of sibling rivalry have a particular resonance), and by drawing attention to a long tradition of reading this as a story of 'types'. Reading the history of how others have read this story is one way of alerting ourselves to the unseen assumptions in our ways of reading. A feminist reading of this text cannot rest content with a reading that reduces these women to 'types' and which makes them oppose one another. Since women are arguably more experienced at being treated as types than men, the traditional readings immediately expose themselves and a new, more liberating, reading is revealed. Every reader of texts knows that texts always come to us bearing with them the history of their own interpretation, and being aware of this history helps us to read the text differently.

The story of the woman bent double (Luke 13.10–17) is another story that does figure in the lectionary and it's something of a feminist classic, a story of a daughter of Abraham! There's not much need to dig very deep into the explicitly feminist toolbox to preach from this text. However, as ever, there is always something more to say than simply that Jesus healed a woman against the inclinations of the religious authorities. Close attention to the text reveals that there is a deeper significance to her being bent double than straightforward physical disability. In biblical terms she cannot 'look up' and therefore she cannot 'look up in hope'. So she stands for all those who have lost hope, all those who can only look down in despair. The story of Jesus bringing her hope and healing is therefore a story that 'looks up' from its own status as a miracle story of one person to become a story of hope for all who are cast down. It might not need feminist theory to spot this, but a preacher who lights with affection and attention on this text is more likely to sense the depth of symbolic meaning and hope in this story.

The last two sermons, on the story of Susanna (chapter 13 of the Greek version of Daniel) and on the parable of the Prodigal Son (Luke 15.11–32), are those that go furthest in rewriting the text so that it speaks with a new voice. These sermons have perhaps learned most from critics like Alicia Suskin Ostriker. The story of Susanna is rarely heard in churches. For many it is outside the canon of Scripture and it is certainly beyond the bounds of the lectionary. However, it is a text that has a strong history of reception, which the sermon, to some extent, explores. It has, ironically, been cited as a story to commend female 'virtue' while many of its depictions have only encouraged male 'sin'! The sermon includes a piece of midrash, a creative retelling of the story that seeks to unsettle the 'morality tale' history which this text has had. The sermon engages with women's experience of desire, scandal and guilt as it seeks to find a new way of speaking of these things. Of course the reading of the story is not offered as a new 'discovery' about the text or a definitive reading of it, but as a means of suggesting a new way of looking at things, through which God might meet us again. You might argue that the sermon on the very familiar parable of the Prodigal Son is actually an attempt to enable the original scandalous force of the parable to be heard again. The sermon does this through another midrashic rewriting of the parable, a rewriting which draws on the experience of women, so notably missing from Luke's original.

Preaching every Sunday demands a great deal of anyone. For anyone alert to the ways in which the Bible has been a powerful agent of the oppression of women there are particular demands, questions and struggles. The Bible is not an innocent text, just as there are no innocent readers or hearers. But there is a whole range of tools, strategies, styles and sources of encouragement for those who want to preach faithfully from the experience of women's lives, and from the standpoint of those who have chosen to resist the oppression of women and to make the world new. From my particular history and life, I have learned to pick up and make use of tools that others have honed for me. I have also learned to believe in my own ability to read a text in a new way, to respond to it in a way that is faithful to my own and to other women's experience and to preach from it with my own voice. I have learned some things in 'the academy', some things in the ordinary places of anyone's life and, most of all, I have learned that these things belong together and that I bring them all to my reading of the Bible and to what I might dare to say from the pulpit on a Sunday. The Bible is a holy book, and I have found that as I have freed myself to read it in as many ways as I can learn, its holiness has shone more brightly and its power to touch my life, and the lives of others, with grace, has grown. I have found that being a feminist biblical scholar by day has proved more fruitful than leaving it to the watches of the night! And my engagement with the Bible has not weakened or lessened, but strengthened in passion and, I pray, wisdom and grace. Amen.

God has no favourites
Mark 7.24–30; James 2.1–7

Jesus had gone away to Tyre. He was in bad need of a holiday
and he'd taken himself 'out of the office'. He was tired of trying
to talk to people who listened only so that they could twist his
words and use them against him. He was fed up to the back teeth
of the disciples who were being so slow to understand what he
had to say and were forever worrying that he was offending
the Pharisees. And he'd had enough of the kind of religion that
thought it was more important to wash your hands at the right
time than to feed the poor or love your neighbour. So he left
for a bit, went off to another region, where he could expect a bit
of peace. He was drained by the effort of sharing a vision that
was always refused. He wanted to hide from malicious looks and
pointing fingers. And he was tired even of his friends. He went
over the border for a change, hoping for a bit of a rest in a place
where nobody would recognize him or expect him to answer
their impossible theological questions or cure their illnesses. And
perhaps some watched him go with a kind of satisfaction, as
though they had seen him off, beaten him for a while. But a
woman from over the border had heard rumours about a rabbi
who could heal the sick and who did not ask for gold in return.
She had heard that he angered the holy men of his own kind
and that he was coming here. So, before he'd even had time to
unpack his suitcase, she fell at his feet and asked him to heal her
daughter. And he, no doubt full of weariness, like one turning
away an unwanted caller at the front door, said that he had to
feed the children first and not the dogs. 'Dogs' was a common
insult that Jews used of Gentiles, and it was not very kind. But
she replied, quick as a flash, that even the dogs can eat the scraps.

Even a tired, even a worn-out rabbi who could only offer her leftovers was something to her and she was determined not to let him off the hook. Weaker mortals would have said, 'Well, if that's your attitude . . .'. And course she shouldn't have been speaking to him at all, in public at that, let alone arguing with him. But she had nothing to lose. And she got her way. Jesus congratulated her on her faith, but it was really her refusal to take no for an answer that did it. And perhaps Jesus knew deep down, from his own reading of the scriptures and from the lessons he had heard in the synagogue, that God did want to bring blessing to all the nations. Among the traditions of the faith which Jesus had learned, was the message that the borders and boundaries with which we live are human creations and that God sees none of them.

The woman was brave, possessed of a hope as strong as the demon that possessed her daughter. Afterwards, Jesus went back to Galilee. He went back the way he had come, back along the road that leads through the hills and down to the lake. And there were more signs still that the God whom Jesus embodied and proclaimed has no favourites, but loves the world and all its people. The voice of the Gentile woman became the key to unlock the doors to a vision of a God who was for all people, all nations.

This is a truly extraordinary story. It's amazing that it ever made it into the Gospels. It's a story that shows Jesus changing his mind. And however convinced most of us are that Jesus was fully human, we still find it strangely disconcerting to have his humanity so bluntly displayed. It's amazing that the Gospel writers record a story that might be seen as a criticism of Jesus, as though he didn't yet understand the will of God. It's amazing because it is a story in which a woman speaks first and in which she wins the argument. There are remarkably few stories like it in the whole of the ancient world. If a teacher loses a debate, it's always a debate with another teacher and not with a disciple, and certainly not with a woman! But in this story, Jesus' own understanding of his mission is changed by a woman, a foreign woman at that, and nothing was ever the same again.

For all that history is not everything, this is one of the stories of Jesus that stands a very high chance of reflecting an actual historical incident. It's hard to imagine why anyone would have wanted to invent it. There was no controversy in the early Church about whether or not Gentiles were to be included in the Church, though there was debate about the terms of their inclusion. And it's hard to think why any disciple of Jesus would have invented such an unflattering story. So it may well be true that Jesus, having once thought of his ministry as only to Israel, and at least partly because of the persistent arguing of a Gentile woman, found himself responding to the needs of a much wider community of people.

Reading this story alongside the passage from the letter of James, makes it all the more remarkable and significant. This letter comes from an early strand of Christianity that was very socially radical, and very strong on Christianity as a new way of behaving and living. The passage we heard begins with a very clear admonition to Christians never to be snobbish, never to treat people differently simply because of the way they look or the amount of money they've got. The writer tells the congregation that if two men come to worship and one is dressed in the finest from Savile Row and the other is pretty obviously a street-sleeper it would be profoundly un-Christian to treat them differently. The writer imagines the door stewards paying special attention to the well-dressed man and offering him a good seat, while telling the poor man he can stand or making sure he stays close to them so that they can keep an eye on him. And I defy anyone not to feel slightly uncomfortable at these words, because what the writer describes is simply the reality of human behaviour. If you've ever been on the receiving end of it you'll know what it feels like, and if you've even been a door steward at church you'll know how you catch yourself thinking. The fascinating thing about the story from the Gospel of Mark is that we find Jesus being very human in this way too, and in some ways we can take that for our comfort.

There are several stories in Mark's Gospel about parents and daughters. Just a couple of chapters before the story of this woman and her daughter is the story of Jairus and his daughter (Mark 5.21–43). If you compare these stories you can see even more clearly how astonishing and significant is the Gospel text for today. Jairus isn't just anybody, he's the president of the synagogue, the session clerk or the church secretary or the chair of the PCC. As Jesus gets off the latest ferry across the lake, Jairus throws himself at Jesus' feet and begs him to come, because his little daughter is at death's door. The text simply tells us that Jesus went with him, accompanied by a great crowd. And, as you all know, Jairus' daughter is healed. That's in chapter 5. But in chapter 7 another parent comes to Jesus, begging him to heal a daughter. But this time, it is not the leader of the synagogue, but a Gentile woman, not someone of importance or status, but a nobody. And Jesus doesn't go immediately. At first he declines. You might say that he does exactly what the letter of James pleads with us not to do.

This is a story of Jesus reacting and behaving as human beings do. He had wanted to do what he could for the leader of the synagogue, who no doubt was a pious and devout as well as an important man. And the Gentile woman had caught him at a moment when he longed more than anything to know that there were limits to his work. And these two stories continue to make an interesting contrast because even in our own experience we read them differently from each other. There is an animated film called *The Miracle Maker* based on the story of Jairus' daughter. I know of a church that has above the altar a stained-glass window depicting her story. It's a story often told. But we hear much less of the other story, of the other little foreign girl at home, possessed of an unclean spirit. Her story is not told in the same way. We distinguish between them to this day. We give one the best seat and the other we keep at the back.

The letter of James is believed to have its roots in the community of Christians which was led from Jerusalem, and in which James, the brother of Jesus, played a leading role. It comes from a community strongly rooted in Jewish traditions, and with a strong emphasis on God's evident love for all people. The writer would evidently have been appalled that any Christian community would welcome the daughter of someone important and turn away the daughter of a stranger. And of course the writer believes this so passionately because he follows Jesus. Because whatever Jesus was tempted on the human level to do, the woman

persuaded him to act in faithfulness to the God whom he proclaimed. And he did heal her daughter. And that little girl, just
like Jairus' daughter, was restored to a new life, and no doubt
there was much rejoicing in her home too.

We all have reason to feel guilty sometimes that we make the
kind of distinctions that make snobs of all of us. And now and
again something will happen to us to bring us up sharp against
the assumptions we've made. In a way, it's reassuring to read
that this was even part of the human experience of someone as
sorted as Jesus. But most of all the story of the Gentile woman
brings the good news of the Gospel to reassure all of us that
Jesus learned and later taught the great truth that God loves all
people, of every nation and tribe. And it is from the knowledge
of that great love, which reaches to all of us, that we shall find
ourselves redeemed from the petty snobberies and pretensions
of human life, for we follow Jesus Christ, in whom God was
present for all people. Thanks be to God. Amen.

The women at the empty tomb
Mark 16.1–8

The end of any book is important. We all like stories to end in a proper way, not necessarily happily, but somehow well. We all have a good sense for an ending. But the Gospel of Mark has a very strange ending. After a long build-up to the story of Jesus' death and then an amazing description of the events of the cross, Mark has a rather short funny paragraph about the resurrection, ending with the words: 'and they said nothing to anyone, for they were afraid' (Mark 16.8).

And that's it. Not even a proper sentence. There are some further verses in the Bibles we have today, but these are very obviously by a different hand and not part of the original, rather as though Jeffrey Archer had added a paragraph to *Pride and Prejudice*. You can tell. Someone thought, as we might, that Mark's Gospel didn't end properly and so they added a few verses themselves, but not many people are convinced. Some people have argued that the writer couldn't possibly have meant to end the Gospel like this, with only one resurrection story and that not even a proper appearance, and only some frightened women who didn't tell anyone! They have imagined Mark being arrested in mid-sentence or dying at his writing desk before the task was completed. But, whatever happened, most people now think that Mark's Gospel does end at this rather strange verse 8. We have lots of stories of the resurrection: the road to Emmaus, Mary Magdalene in the garden, the disciples behind closed doors, Jesus cooking fish on the beach, but not one of them is in Mark's Gospel. There is only this one story about some startled women reduced to silence.

Rather as Basil Brush used to protest to Mr Derek, it seems impossible to think you could leave the story there. Well, for a start, if the women really did never say anything to anyone, how did anyone get to hear what had happened, and how was the story ever told? How did the Gospel writer himself even know that Jesus had risen? And why on earth were the women afraid? They weren't afraid to stand and watch a crucifixion, they weren't afraid to go and tend to a three-day-old body, they weren't afraid to contemplate opening a grave, so why should some good news faze them when so much bad had not discouraged them? Why were they afraid? And why were they silent?

Of course, for us, speaking out about the faith is part of our expectation of what good Christians do. We remember very well the ending of Matthew's Gospel in which Jesus tells us to go and make disciples of all nations (Matthew 28.19–20). You couldn't do that in silence. And we remember the end of Luke's Gospel when Jesus tells us to go and be his witnesses, armed with power from above (Luke 24.45–49). And the end of John's Gospel tells us that there is so much to say about Jesus that if you wrote it all down the world couldn't hold the books that would be written (John 21.25). But what about Mark's end, in silence?

Silence is an important theme in Mark's Gospel, not just at the end, but throughout the whole book. Think of all those stories when Jesus tells people to keep silent, not to let out the secret. A leper, a blind man, the disciples at the Transfiguration, all told to keep silent. But it's interesting that Jesus never tells any women to keep silent. He healed Peter's mother-in-law, he healed the woman with haemorrhages, he healed the daughter of the Syro-Phoenician woman, but he didn't tell any of them to keep silent. This might seem strange to us. Why silence the men and not the women? We live in a culture where women are always being chided for gossiping or for talking too much, where it's assumed that women talk. But it was different for Jesus. He lived at a time when women did not speak in public. In private of course, but never in public. Women then were like children in Victorian times, seen but not heard. So Jesus did not need to tell them to be silent. He knew that they would be anyway. He had to tell the men to keep their lips sealed, but not the women. Women were used to silence.

We can see it in other parts of the New Testament too, where it's assumed that women should be silent. The first letter of Paul to Timothy, for example, says, 'Let a woman learn in silence with full submission. I permit no woman to teach or to have authority over a man; she is to keep silent' (1 Timothy 2.12). Such ideas seem very strange to us today, but Jesus lived and breathed in such a world. He didn't need to tell the women to be quiet about him, because he knew that they would be quiet about everything. In very few of the stories in Mark's Gospel does a woman say anything. A woman anoints Jesus with precious ointment and it is Jesus who tells us what her action means. A poor widow puts two tiny coins in the Temple collection box, but Jesus speaks to us about her. The women stand silently around the cross, but the male centurion is the one who speaks. The women are silent and that's how everyone thought it should be. Until the resurrection.

So we shouldn't be surprised that the women were silent and afraid when they found the tomb empty and heard the words of the young man in white. They weren't afraid because they had seen a terrible or awesome sight. They weren't particularly shy or timid women. But they were afraid to speak out because they weren't used to it. They were simply afraid of public speaking as many women still are. They knew that it wasn't done for women to speak out, to preach sermons or to make speeches. They knew that few of the Romans or their countrymen would want to lend ears to some preaching women. They were afraid to speak. They were afraid because women were not usually told to speak. Until the resurrection.

Until the resurrection. Then the dead culture of the past was overturned. Then the dead are given new life, the sick are healed and the silent are stirred into speech. In the past, women had been silent, men had spoken foolishly, truth had been twisted, cruel and bitter pain had been endured. But after the resurrection things were different. Everything was made new, every man and every woman could be reborn, set free from old slaveries, born again. Everything is turned upside down. In the story up to now the men had been silenced and the women left in their familiar silence. Now the pattern is broken, and not just by letting the men speak. Instead, with a shock that is terrifying and unfamiliar, the women are charged with speech. Christ is not dead! Christ is risen! The word of God is given for us to speak, even to be placed on the lips of women. The silence at last is broken! All creation sings its praise to the Risen One!

Except of course that it's not so simple. People who have been broken, silenced and afraid find it very hard to leave behind their brokenness. Christ has come to open up the tombs in which we all live, to set us free to live new lives. But like these frightened women we cling just a bit to the old familiar life. It is as though God opens the cage door, but we are afraid to come out into freedom, because there are inner chains that bind us still. And these are far harder to break or unlock. God has told us in Christ that we are forgiven and free. But we still cling to feelings of unworthiness. God had told us in Christ that death is defeated, but we are still afraid. God has told us in Christ that we are born again, but we still feel once born. The angel told the women they could speak, but they were still scared to open their mouths, so scared they couldn't do it. Like all of us, they found it hard to believe good news.

There are many stories about women, silence and speaking. Maya Angelou is the wonderful woman poet who wrote a poem for President Clinton's first inauguration. She is black and beautiful and sassy, but her brave freedom has been won from a life of many struggles and tragedies. When she was a girl she was raped by a family friend and he told her that she mustn't tell. But she could not hide the signs of the violence she suffered and he was brought to justice. Maya was so traumatized by all this that she became silent for several years. She believed that her speech was dangerous, that her very breath might poison people. But she began to talk again when another woman introduced her to the beauty and power of words as she read authors like Dickens aloud to her. And maybe you have seen the film *The Piano* in which a young Scottish woman refuses to speak and communicates by writing notes. The only sounds she wants to make are the notes of her piano. But when the piano is finally plunged into the sea, she finds her voice again. In the fairy tale, the little mermaid exchanges her voice for a pair of human legs, but her silent beauty fails to win the prince and she finally becomes only foam upon the waves. Silence is not the way to life.

The women in the Bible are no less caught up in themes of silence and speech. And it is no accident that it is the grave that is universally the place of silence. There is nowhere as silent as the grave. The women have come to the tomb of Jesus, not to make speeches, but simply in the silence of death to anoint a voiceless body. But they are dumbfounded when the angel tells them that Christ is risen and that, at last, they must speak. The old ways are no more. From death has come life. From the silence has come speech. From the grave comes the living word of God.

Of course the women were afraid. Even death is sometimes more comfortable than a radical change and a new beginning. No doubt they found it hard to believe that they really did have a voice, a gospel to proclaim, good news to shout to the world. Mark tells us they told no one. Matthew (28.8) says they told Peter and the disciples, but then left the public proclamation to the men. And so it was that women were the seers, but men the speakers. But the gospel of the resurrection is that all the old tombs, all the old slaveries, all the old captivities are now left behind. Few of us could blame the women for being so timid. For are we not the same? We hear the words of the gospel, that Christ is risen, that death is no more, that evil is defeated, and we cannot quite trust ourselves to believe it. We hardly dare to believe that God loves us, that Christ is our Saviour, that the Spirit gives life. Sometimes even we prefer the comfortable deaths we die each day or the same reliable cynicisms or the same familiar self-doubts. But the angel of resurrection comes to stir our silence into speech, our death to life, our despair to hope.

So, men and women, do not be afraid. Fearing nothing and believing the good news of the resurrection, you will know that this story is not your end, but your new beginning. If Mark has few resurrection stories, then we will add our own, as here in this community and in many other places, the silent, the dying, the miserable, the wicked and the wounded, find that life is made new.

Christ is risen! Alleluia! Amen!

Jephthah's daughter
Judges 11.29–40

Oxford is a place full of stories for children. Alice lived in Wonderland, but also in Oxford. C. S. Lewis wrote the magical stories of Narnia here. And now Oxford is the home of a famous reading tree, and of Philip Pullman's Lyra. The traditional Oxford might seem a rather un-child-friendly place, but behind the stone walls and the neat gardens are all these signs that Oxford has its own world for children. Since time began grown-up people have given much thoughtfulness to the way in which we care for our children. And this is not only the concern of those who are actually themselves parents. It's something that might be, and ought to be, the care of us all. In our own culture there is a good deal of thinking going on about what it means to be a child, what rights and freedoms children should have, how they should be treated and cared for, and what might be expected of them. No generation has found this easy. We live with a deep fear that they might be abducted or abused. We worry that they are become too precocious, expected to be adult too soon, not allowed to be children. We worry that they become, far too early, participants in consumerism, with even their play being influenced by business and advertising. We find ourselves appalled at what past generations have sometimes done to children, but we continue to struggle ourselves with knowing what kind of a society we want for them to live in, and indeed, what a kind of a society grown-ups might live in. As people who know we belong to another world as well as this one, we need to know what it means to bring up the children in our community so that they can catch some of the life of this God's world too, sense something of the holiness of God, and begin to follow the one we follow, Jesus.

39

We want to know how we can give our children to God, or perhaps it's more that we want to give God to our children, for them to know the love of God and to flourish and grow in goodness all their days.

Because this is how *we* are, we may sometimes find it oddly comforting to know that others have struggled before us with the same quest. They may have found different solutions and puzzled in different ways, but we can find something of a sense of solidarity with them and a sense of their oneness with us. We can recognize, in stories often very ancient and far from us, the power of human love for a child, the joy of knowing a child, the sorrow of losing one. In these things we sing and we bleed as they did. The story of Jephthah and his daughter may seem a very distant story indeed, a bit of the Bible best consigned to the marginal, a story to be passed over. But, as is so often true, a pause to read it carefully will open for us the very issues with which we struggle too. And in these ancient words, dusty with history and neglect, we may yet learn something of the mercy and love of God.

The story comes right in the heart of the book of Judges. Jephthah has been appointed to lead the army of Israel against the Ammonites. He has something of a past, so he's hoping that victory will renew his standing with Israel. So he makes one of those bargains with God. He says something like, 'God, if you'll give me victory, the first creature I meet afterwards I'll burn as a sacrifice to you.' And Jephthah gets his victory. But who should be the first creature to come out and greet him, dancing and playing her tambourine, but his daughter, his only child. He is beside himself with a Midas-like sorrow but Jephthah knows that he can't go back on a vow to God, and even his daughter agrees with him. And the Bible text says that 'he did with her according to the vow he had made' (Judges 11.39). Just like that. It's a terrible story indeed, one to make you turn away from a God who could demand such a thing, who could enter into such a bargain or make a father keep it. But the Bible text is not quite as straightforward as that. When you read it closely you can see that there is another story trying to get out. The narrator tells us that she was a virgin who had never slept with a man, and then there are some very strange verses about the daughter being allowed a reprieve so that she can mourn the fact that she is never going to get married. It was some medieval Jewish scholars who noticed that there could be another story here, that perhaps Jephthah did not kill his daughter, but dedicated her to perpetual virginity. Behind this strange 'pick your own ending' phenomenon lay a struggle in the community about God and children. At one stage the people of Israel stood out among their neighbours because they rejected child sacrifice. They refused to treat their children like that, or to believe that God could want that. They dedicated their children to God, but in very different ways. In the eighteenth century, Handel wrote a wonderful oratorio based on this story. People come away from performances saying that Handel, or his librettist, has changed the biblical ending, making it happier because the daughter doesn't die as she does in the Bible. But actually the two readings are already there in the Bible itself, as people long ago struggled to know what it was that God wanted them to do with their children.

It would be tempting of course to say that, however you read this story in Judges, we have come a long way since then. Child sacrifice is not on our agenda. And, we no longer want to argue that living like a nun is a more godly life for a girl. We no longer believe that the God we have seen in Jesus Christ wants the sacrifice of our children, or that God will take any part in bargains like Jephthah's. But perhaps the story, with its uncertainness and ambiguity, will encourage us not to be complacent, but to wonder how we ourselves are doing in what we offer our children. And we might reflect too on what it means to offer our children to God or to offer God to them.

Of course it is never exactly a question of us giving our children to God at all. The truth is that our children are a gift to us from God. Gifts are not always easy to receive and they can be a huge responsibility. They don't come to everyone in the same way, but they are gifts all the same. The children we have in our communities and our families are not for us to bargain with or to live our own lives through, but they are those who have been given to us to receive with joy and thanksgiving. It's striking that Jesus believed that there was something about children which meant they were closer to the Kingdom than the best-behaved adults. There is something about the children among us that can point us readily and easily to God. It might not feel like that when they won't let you sleep or they're behaving like monsters, but there is something about the way in which children simply are which makes them parables of the Kingdom. They come to us as gift. Not all of us may want to be or be fortunate to be parents, but all of us can have the privilege of knowing and meeting children, and seeing in them this gift of God.

It's also the gospel, according to Jesus, that God's purpose for all children, for all people, is that they grow into fullness of life. In Christ he chose us before the world was founded, to be dedicated, to be without blemish in his sight, to be full of love. Baptism is about new life in Christ, but perhaps it's better to say it's about a full life, about the promise and hope that this new member of the Church will have fullness of life. And that means, not that he or she will have great wealth or success or even length of days, but that whatever he does and wherever she goes, this child will know the love of God, know the true welcome of a human community, live a holy life of generosity and love towards others, and be blessed in the fullest sense. Being part of the Christian family and receiving God's blessing is not about receiving a holy kind of 'luck', but of being part of a community of people who are trying to follow a particular way of life, a way modelled for us by Jesus himself, and looking for a particular hope, for a world marked by justice, peace and gracious generosity.

Today we pray for all the children we know and for the children in our society and in our world, and we long for a world in which no child shall ever be sacrificed to the gods, to a parent's ambition, to economic greed, to slavery or to consumerism. Let us receive children as a gift from God with gratitude and grace, and give thanks that God receives all of us into the family of God's children. Amen.

Salome
Mark 6.17–29

You might think the story of the beheading of John the Baptist an unpromising text for a baptismal service. It might, I suppose, serve to remind us that baptism has real, even political consequences. It's about proclaiming justice and risking everything for the sake of truth. John the Baptist never compromised, always refused to bow before the corrupt authority of the state, and spoke the words of a prophet until his dying day. If you need to convince yourself that baptism is much, much more than a nice social occasion, then look to the Baptist.

But today I want to look at the story of Salome, the daughter of Herodias who danced before Herod and asked for the head of the Baptist on a dish. Because the story, and what has happened to it since, is a good example of what can happen to a girl; her life, her reputation, her name. We know that this girl is called Salome, but not because the Gospel tells us. We know it from the Jewish historian Josephus, but we assume he was right and anyway, it has stuck.

One of the less offensive things King Herod Antipas did was to run away with his brother's wife. I won't go into some of his more offensive ones lest I put you off your lunch. But it was for this mix of adultery and incest that John the Baptist gave Herod a hard time. This did not, naturally enough, make Herodias, Herod's new wife, a big fan, and she wanted to be rid of him. But Herod, having at least a tiny bit of political sense, knew it would not be a vote winner. So he just kept the Baptist stewing in prison. Then Herod held a birthday party. He had to throw it himself, presumably because there was no one else who wanted to throw it for him, and one of the guests was Herodias' daughter by her first marriage. So she was Herod's step-daughter and his niece at the same time. As it turned out, she was a fantastic dancer; Ginger Rogers, Cyd Charisse and perhaps a touch of Darcey Bussell thrown in. Herod, perhaps more than a bit tipsy on the birthday booze, was so taken by her dancing that he offered her anything she wanted, even half his kingdom. Since she already had everything a girl could want, she asked her mother what she thought. And Mother suggested the head of John the Baptist. Salome went back and told Herod, adding for good measure and for memorable effect that she would like it served on a plate. The Gospel tells us that a soldier did the deed, handed her the plate and that she passed it on pretty fast to her mother, and it's not hard to see why. And at that point Salome disappears from the record. One can only hope that she thought twice about taking her mother's advice in future, and that she learned that even when you have cut the head off a prophet, that doesn't mean you'll never hear of him again.

It's the not the sort of thing any of us would want to happen to our daughters, and you have to admit that Herodias would never have won Mother of the Year award. She used her daughter and got her mixed up in the most horrible and grisly vendetta. It's a nasty story. But of course, the story has got worse as it has been retold, and retold it has been many, many times. In the Gospel account, Salome is an abused innocent. There is nothing in the text that tells us directly that her dance was deliberately provocative and we can see that it's her mother who is the driving force. But as the story gets retold, poor Salome changes into a terrible femme fatale. It shouldn't happen to any girl. But it does. Even by the Middle Ages, Salome had been turned into an erotic dancer. Apparently, you can find her on the doors of a church in Verona, her dancing body in a sinuous line, almost like a snake. And she is over the door of the great cathedral in Rouen, where the artist imagines her dancing on her hands and so inviting the male gaze. She is the voluptuous virago, in contrast with the 'good women' of medieval Christianity. But Salome really came into the public gaze at the turn of the last century where she cropped up almost everywhere. A play by Oscar Wilde, a novella by Flaubert (*Hérodiade*), an opera all her own by Strauss, and even a painting by Klimt. There she is, and becoming more and more sinister. Salome comes to be immoral, dangerous and anti-religion. Look what they have done to this poor child! Oscar Wilde even has it that she was only out for revenge because John the Baptist spurned her approaches. In Mark's Gospel, she is just a girl, the apple of Herod's eye. But Salome goes wild in the hands of Oscar, and she is monstrous indeed, a devil in a woman's frame. It shouldn't happen to a girl. How can it be that innocence is so easily turned to wickedness, that falsehood so easily beguiles? It is not what we want for our daughters, or for our sons.

In the Gospel of Mark, the name Salome is found twice, though neither time is it used of the daughter of Herodias. We find it at the end of the Gospel, when the author describes the women who gathered at the foot of the cross and the women who went to the tomb, very early on the first day of the week. He tells us that there were two Marys and a Salome in this faithful group. Now Salome who danced before Herod was not the same Salome who appears later as one of the women disciples of Jesus, or at least it is so very improbable that I would eat my hat if it were true. But, perhaps it is interesting nonetheless that the Gospel offers us two Salomes, two women's lives. It is sad, but true, that the life of the innocent dancer turned femme fatale is the one that fascinates the artists and playwrights, while the faithful disciple leaves only her name behind and little more. Evil and wickedness are somehow always more fascinating to us than simple goodness. But today, the Salomes of the Gospel offer us a choice. Will we choose evil or will we choose good? Will we play a part in or go along with evil and terror, like one Salome, or will we be faithful to God, like the other Salome? And what will we give to our daughters and our sons; death or life, evil or good, falsehood or truth? Will we turn them from innocents into viragos or will we move heaven and earth to show them the ways of a holy God? Today, of course, we have made promises to God that the baby girl, Katherine, whom we have baptized, is set on the path to discipleship and that we will do all we can, with God's grace, to help her walk the path of life, goodness, beauty and joy.

Of course, in a perfect preacher's world, she would have been called Salome. But the name Katherine is also one which has a history and which offers some choices and possibilities. There is Catherine of Alexandria, a woman of great learning who was martyred for her faith. There's Catherine of Genoa, a dreamy saint full of visions and ideas. And there's Catherine of Siena, who was known for her spirituality, her devotion to God and for her gift in reconciling people to one another and to God. Or, on the other hand, there's Catherine of Medici, a tyrant queen of France who specialized in the massacre of Protestants! But, of course, this Katherine will be herself. It is our hope and prayer today that, whatever she is, whatever she does, however long her life, however deep her loves, she will be a disciple of Jesus Christ and a faithful member of the Church. We pray that, though like the disciple Salome before her she will know pain and sorrow, she will also know the joy of resurrection and life. We pray that when her story is told by future generations, it will be said of her that she knew the things of God. And this can be our hope, and not our certainty. We cannot write our children's stories for them, and perhaps just as well. But we can tell our stories to her and tell her the great story by which we live our lives, the story of God's love for us in Jesus Christ.

From early times the Church has received the children of believers by baptism so that with help and support they may grow up in Christ, and by the grace of God serve Christ all their days. For all our children, so full of promise, and for the gifts of God that have already been given to them, we offer thanks and praise. May they dance with joy, live with kindness and mercy, and know the love of God. Amen.

Mary and Martha
Luke 10.38–42

When a mature student says, 'I have been a Martha all my life and now I am going to be a Mary,' we all know what she means. After years of looking after (maybe) a man, a house and children she's going to develop her mind and do some studying. In putting her life in those terms, of Martha and Mary, she demonstrates a popular reading of the story. We have all learned to interpret this story in a particular way. But more than that, we've all learned to interpret our own lives in particular ways.

I think most of us, if we have heard this story before, have grown up with the view that Martha is not the one to be admired, whereas Mary is. Whenever Martha is portrayed in paintings or hymns, or anything at all really, she is earthy, plump, in that very telling phrase 'just a housewife', interrupting, even nagging. She breathes cooking and she smells of the kitchen. Whereas Mary is thin, beautiful, quiet and attentive. I heard someone say once that, as a child, she always felt rather sorry for anyone called Martha. Mary and Martha have become 'types', and many women have a clear sense of which type they are. Most women have learned that it is not good to be a 'Martha', or at least it is not 'the better part'. And throughout most of Christian tradition Martha has had a rough ride. Since most women do find themselves at least for part of their lives doing 'housewifely' practical things, this seems very unfair. We find ourselves pressed into 'service', but then told that this is not the 'better part'. You just can't win.

For much of the Church's life, Mary and Martha were taken to be types of two different kinds of life: the active life of the world with all its cares and labours, and the contemplative life of prayer and quiet and study. Mary was the type of the contemplative, the quiet nun-like one who sat absorbed in single-minded attention at Jesus' feet. Martha represented all those who could not live the Christian life with complete serenity and commitment because they had so many other things to think about. Martha was made the patron saint of housekeepers and cooks, and the few churches dedicated to her are on pilgrim routes where hospitality is offered to weary travellers. And you needn't think that this changed at the Reformation. In fact if anything it got worse. Apparently, for Martin Luther, the two sisters from Bethany were the types for two different approaches to salvation, one true and the other false (see Moltmann-Wendel, 1990). Martha represented those who wrongly believed that they could be saved by their works, and Mary those who knew that it was only by the grace of Jesus Christ that they would find life. Luther believed that Martha's work would be counted as nothing and that God wanted only the work of Mary. So poor Martha got an even lower rating than before! And people who work hard with their hands or who labour in service in the home felt and maybe still feel even more devalued, though I'm left thinking that someone must have done the cooking, even for the holiest of Catholic monks or the most studious of Protestant divines. This story is not fair to Martha. We know, from Luke's Gospel, that Jesus relied upon well-to-do women like her to keep him going, fed and rested. How would it have been if all his hosts had asserted their right to leave the cooking pots and sit at his feet? Who would have prepared the Last Supper, for a start? And then, is Mary really so wonderful, sitting quietly submissive? Is that really a good model for a liberated woman? And I'm not much more impressed by the later view that women could do best in life by combining the gifts of a Martha and a Mary.

But the history of this story is saved by some of those who encourage us to read it differently. And, what's even more important, they are also those who encourage us to read our own lives differently. Stereotypes are damaging things. There is a quite different and challenging interpretation of this story that comes from, of all people, John Calvin. Calvin thought that it wasn't right to see Martha and Mary as types or, as we might put it, stereotypes. He wrote, 'Now this passage has been wickedly perverted to commend what is called the contemplative life. But if we aim at bringing out the genuine sense, it will appear that Christ was far from intending that His disciples should devote themselves to idle and frigid speculation' (quoted by Loveday Alexander, 1992, p. 174).

Calvin was driven to challenge the popular reading of the story, the one we're all used to, because he believed that the world of daily work was a good world and the place in which Christian life was most often actually lived. How could it be then that Jesus could have despised it? Calvin solved the dilemma by arguing that Mary and Martha were not stereotypes or examples, but actual, real women. The story wasn't about different lifestyles, but about choosing when to act and be busy and when to sit still and listen and think. It's not a question of posing action and contemplation against each other, but of knowing when it's appropriate to do which. He points out that Mary was hardly going to sit at Jesus' feet for the whole of her life! And none of us are stereotypes either. We all have it in us to be both active and passive, to be thinkers and doers. God wants us to live lives marked by wholeness and harmony, not by identities that deny all that we can do and be. God wants all of us sometimes to be active and sometimes to be quiet. Sometimes God calls us to prayer and sometimes to revolution, sometimes to pray for the poor, and sometimes to feed them, sometimes to exercise our bodies and sometimes to exercise our souls, sometimes to debate an issue and sometimes to get out there and do something about it. Jesus was not, in this story, establishing a permanent hierarchy of values between one lifestyle and another. Jesus actually gave us very few general rules. Instead he liked to tell stories and say things to upset the expectations of his hearers, and Luke was the Gospel writer who particularly enjoyed telling us those stories.

One way to recover this story is to try to read it as the original hearers or readers might have done, although that's a very difficult thing to do. They would have been used to stories about sibling rivalry. It was a common kind of story. Jesus often told such stories. Think of the parable of the prodigal son. The elder brother asks, as Martha does, 'Is it fair?' And the thing about

Martha is that, just like the elder brother, she does all the right things. Those who first heard this story would have known that offering hospitality and doing 'much serving' were very positive things indeed. Jesus even calls himself a servant in this Gospel. By all that anyone has been led to expect, Martha is in the right. But, the thing about Jesus, in story after story, is that he is remarkably unconcerned about who is in the right and who is in the wrong. He tells us again and again that doing all the right things is not necessarily what God is interested in. You can serve others, have concern for the poor, keep all the commandments, but, as he says to the rich young ruler, one thing is needful, the will to follow Christ without counting the cost. The Pharisee might fast the right number of times and do all the right things, but it's the repentant publican whom God loves. God continues to upset the applecart, until we realize that it's not the applecart that is important at all! God persists in loving those who don't do the right things. And of course, the gospel of God's love for sinners is not a recommendation that we all become sinners! Because Jesus praised Mary it doesn't mean that we should all abandon practical service. But the gospel means that we come to know a different kind of God, and we learn, what we need to learn again and again, that God loves us not for the good points we earn, but just because God can't help loving us. We need not be anxious, as Martha was, because there is one thing needful, to hear the gospel and to know that God loves us and accepts us.

And, for the sake of Martha, and for all women and men, it's important to know that Martha was more than her stereotype and that there is another story about Martha in the New Testament. This story is in John's Gospel. Her brother, Jesus' friend Lazarus, has died. It is Martha, again the active one, who goes out to meet Jesus when he finally arrives. And she berates him because if he had been here earlier Lazarus would have lived. But then, and even before Lazarus is raised, she confesses her faith in Christ by saying 'I believe that you are the Messiah, the Son of God' (John 11.27), a confession every bit as profound as Peter's more famous one. The Church was built on Peter's confession, but it was also built on Martha's. Like an apostle, she is a bearer of faith and a pillar of the Church. Not the sour-faced *Hausfrau* later tradition has made her, but a woman of faith. Like Peter, both practical and devout.

So what does this story say for us today? I think it calls us to resist the urge to stereotype one another or ourselves or to value one kind of life more than another. There is a time for us all to be practical and a time for us all to be thoughtful. For some of us one may come more easily than the other, but it's important not to lock ourselves into one way of being. We should expect to see professors in the kitchen and cooks in the pulpit, to see philosophers protesting at the G8 summit and builders on their knees at prayer. We should expect everyone here, and in any church, to be developing the whole breadth of their experience and personality. And we should all be learning the wisdom to discern when to get down on our knees to pray and when to roll up our sleeves to do something. There is room in every church for Mary and Martha and room in every church for Mary to cook and Martha to pray. But, even more than that, the story proclaims the gospel that says God is not nearly as interested as we are in who's doing the right thing or the wrong thing, that God continues to love the ones we despise or criticize or reject or value hardly at all. And that God loves you and me, when we get it right and when, inevitably, we get it wrong.

Perhaps now we need to tell the story differently. As Mary sits at Jesus' feet, listening to his teaching, she suddenly says, 'Jesus, my sister Martha is busying herself in practical things. Tell her to come and sit here with us, so that she can listen to you as I do.' And Jesus says, 'Leave her alone. She is doing what is best. It shall not be taken away from her.' Amen.

Bent double
Luke 13.10–17

Fay Weldon's drama, *Big Women*, took us back to the beginnings of the second wave of feminism in the 1970s. Here were women being big and brash, ready to change the world, strong, defiant, iconoclastic. Until the moment when one of them recognizes with terrible agony that her break for freedom has cost her her own children. Two tiny boys taunt her as 'the witch' and she, the biggest of the big women, is bent double with tears and despair. Inside every big woman, there is a small woman, bent double. And inside every man too there is something which can bend them double and from which they (you) need healing and restoring.

If I could paint a picture of this week it would be a picture of many people, men and women, bent double. Picture an old man, near to death, shrunken and small, bent now in his bed into a foetal position until death comes to bring him the peace and rest which God brings at the end of a long and fulfilled life. Picture a man in prison, his neck still bearing the marks of the strip of the blanket with which he tried to hang himself. He sits hunched in the prison visiting room, his head bent as he looks at the floor hardly able to speak he is so filled with despair. Picture a priest standing looking sorrowfully at the burned ruins of his church, his head bent in sorrow and anger that such things can happen, the statue of Mary scorched by the flames. Picture a girl shielding herself from the blows as her stepfather bludgeons her to death, bent double by his ferocious anger. Picture a woman grieving at her child's death, bending over her own knees to comfort herself with the clasp of her own body. Picture a young refugee woman distraught beyond measure because her boyfriend has killed himself after a row with her. Sometimes it may seem as though all God's people are bent double, burdened by griefs too hard to bear, carrying a heavier load than anyone ever should. Here we are, O Lord, standing in need of prayer. Who will come to raise us up and save us?

Maybe Luke's story of the woman bent double will speak to us. It takes place on the Sabbath. All activity is prohibited. You are not supposed to do anything except pray and read the scriptures. You are not even supposed to heal anyone. Even doctors need a day off. Jesus is teaching in one of the synagogues. He is a popular preacher and there is a full congregation today. He has prepared well and he is in full swing. It's good to listen to. But then Jesus interrupts his own sermon because he has seen a woman who needs healing. She is bent double with some kind of paralysis. It's so bad that she can't even look up. He calls her to him and heals her. And she stands up straight. She begins to praise God. Who wouldn't? She's been bent double for eighteen years. Eighteen years she has spent looking at the floor, looking at other people's feet, and now she stands straight and tall and she can raise her eyes and look the preacher and just about anyone else in the eye! You'd think this might be the climax to any sermon, and that the congregation might join in her singing. But not a bit of it. Some of the members of the congregation are fidgeting and the president of the synagogue, the church secretary if you like, is looking really put out. They're paying a good preaching fee. They were enjoying the sermon. They didn't expect it to be interrupted. But he's too polite to complain to the visiting preacher. Instead he stands up and tells the congregation that there are six working days, so they can come and be cured on one of them, not on the Sabbath. But of course, he's not really concerned about healing them. The doors of the synagogue might well be locked on the other days and Jesus will be preaching somewhere else. And anyway, the woman didn't come to pester the preacher, and she was as surprised as anyone by what had happened. The synagogue president was just annoyed because the order of the service had been interrupted. But Jesus sees through him. He shouts at him and all those like him, 'You hypocrites! Does not each of you on the Sabbath untie his ox or his donkey from the manger, and lead it away to give it water? And ought not this woman, a daughter of Abraham whom Satan bound for eighteen long years, be set free from this bondage on the Sabbath day?' (Luke 13.15–16). Most of the people cheer him to the skies. They know words of God when they hear them. And what is religion for, if it's not for healing what is broken and lifting up the down-cast and saving the oppressed? Religion isn't about preserving holy rituals and keeping worship just so. It's about fulfilling the mission of God. We come to worship God so that we can find the grace and strength to be saved and to hold others up. When the niceties of worship or church bureaucracy come before the kingdom of God, then we are hypocrites. God help us if any person bent double by grief or sorrow finds us too absorbed in the running of the Church to offer comfort. God help any of us if we turn to the people of God in our need and find them fussing over little things. God help us.

And this small story in Luke's Gospel is even more profound than it seems on first reading. The woman is not simply an old worshipper, tormented by gout or arthritis, the way she is often portrayed. The fact that she cannot look up also means that she has no hope, that she can't raise her head and see the approach of redemption. This is the same Gospel writer who has Jesus say to the disciples, 'Stand up and raise your heads, because your redemption is drawing near' (Luke 21.28). Now this woman stands straight and tall, with no more weary knees or tired hands. And she can look, she can look for redemption. She can look in hope. She has gained an upright walk and a future. And Jesus calls her a 'daughter of Abraham'. There are plenty of 'sons of Abraham', but now, Jesus says, the daughters also share in the hope and the promise that was given all those years ago to Abraham. Now your sons and your daughters will dream dreams. Now your sons and your daughters will claim the promises of God.

The Sabbath law was always a law of liberation. When you think about how hard it has been and still is for the most vulnerable workers to get good working conditions, fair wages, time off, protection and rights, it is amazing that in the ancient world there was such a strong command that no one, not even slaves, should work all the time. The Sabbath law was a law of liberation, to bring rest and healing and restoration to the weary. We have become so used to associating the Sabbath law with hard-line rigour that we have forgotten what liberation and freedom it first brought. The Sabbath rest was not a restriction, but a freedom. When Jesus healed the woman he was actually fulfilling the liberating intention of the Sabbath! For her it was going to be the first Sabbath for eighteen years that she could really enjoy! She is a true daughter of Abraham and, at last, she can fully share in the blessing promised to him and his children, his sons and his daughters.

What of us here? Are we truly sons and daughters of Abraham, our eyes raised looking in hope for the coming of God's kingdom? Are we ready to receive the grace of God that brings hope to the most sorrowful of souls? Are we ready to proclaim and celebrate the liberating love of God for all God's people, even if it sometimes interrupts our ordered lives? I am more proud this week than I have ever been that a charity to support asylum seekers has found a place in our building. Even if it does inconvenience us it is one place when those bent double are finding hope. This week at the church meeting we will also discuss welcoming a small and vulnerable group of Christians to use our hall for their worship. Every Friday a group of people who live with the alcohol addiction of their loved ones meet here to gather strength and hope from one another. Every day, through prayer and talking and over cups of tea, you people of this congregation offer comfort and support to one another. When we are bent double, there are people who will help us to raise our eyes in hope. Many of you in your daily lives and in your work offer such hope to others, often not caring of the time or the day, but just bringing healing and hope wherever it is needed and wherever it may be found.

So I would like to paint another picture of this week. It has all those pictures of the people bent double still there. But they are in gentle, pale colours, their outlines fading. And splashed across them are different pictures in bright and vivid colours of people finding new life. I see a man leaving detention. I see a church in the middle of a grey housing estate filled with vivid and sweet-smelling flowers. I see a group of elders dancing in the pews. I see a garden being tended and growing and offering its beauty to many friends. I see a baby about to be born. I see hope coming into tired lives and joy even among the poor and destitute. I see in many places, expected and unexpected, those who were bent double raising their eyes in hope. God has heard our prayers. Sometimes still we are bent with pain and sorrow. But never is there a time when we cannot look up and wait for redemption and never is there a time when we shall lose hope that it will come.

The Church is here to be a sign of that hope. If there is anything that prevents us from doing that then we should cast it out. The Spirit of the Lord is upon us and has called us to set free the oppressed, to set free the captives, to comfort the broken-hearted, to make straight all who are bent double, to raise them up so that they can stand straight and look up in hope. This is our mission, for women and for men. And God will heal and strengthen us for this task. Amen.

Susanna
Chapter 13 of the
Greek version of Daniel

When I first went to university I was one of a very small number of women in my college. The rather charming concession that the college made to our presence was to put full-length mirrors in each of our rooms. The college had apparently learned that women like to be looked at, even by themselves, that women like 'putting on appearances'. However, this truth was rather belied by the number of young men who knocked at my door and asked would I mind if they used the mirror! That aside, the ten mirrors were very significant.

In the Christ Church Picture Gallery in Oxford there is a picture called *The Vanity Of Mary Magdalene*. It is a very beautiful picture. It shows Mary surrounded by the tools of vanity; combs and brushes and, most importantly, a mirror. The spectator looks on and is presumably supposed to disapprove, and to feel the force of the lesson that vanity and pride in beauty are unworthy things and that they were well put behind her when Mary repented and became a disciple. But, what the spectator also does it to admire the beauty of a desirable woman. She is painted with her hair down, glossy and shining as though just washed in Timotei. She has obviously been to the Renaissance equivalent of Bravissimo and her eyes hint at the kind of things that girls hint at on page three. So the painting says one thing and does another. It says that vanity and lust are bad, that the Magdalene was a sinner for making herself beautiful, but what it does is enable the spectator to enjoy her beauty and even to engage in the kind of lustful looking which the title of the painting seems to condemn. She is criticized for looking at herself in the mirror, but we enjoy looking at her through the one-way mirror of the canvas.

The story of Susanna is one of the most often depicted stories in the Bible. Of course, the painted scene is always the same one; Susanna taking her bath with the elders peering at her. And the irony is that we, the viewers of the painting, are peering at her too. It's like the Christ Church painting, full of irony. At one level, the message is that the elders who hid so that they could watch her naked are nothing more than dirty old men. But the paintings turn us into dirty old men too as we, unseen, watch her bathing. We join the elders to spy on Susanna taking her bath. In some of the paintings she looks back at us looking at her, in a way which might make us ashamed, if we are honest. Susanna has not really been protected by those who have painted her. The painters make little of condemning the peeping toms in the bushes. Instead they only reproduce with their brushes the object of the elders' gaze, Susanna's flesh. Her body represents and mirrors not Susanna herself, but their lust and desire. And her innocence becomes hinted guilt as her body communicates and explains the elders' lust. The painters make us want to look at this beautiful body and they hint that it is displayed almost willingly. They persuade us that this is seduction, that Susanna likes being looked at. And sometimes Susanna doesn't look at us at all. Instead she looks at herself, in a mirror (see Berger, 1972, p. 50). She enjoys looking at herself. She was asking for it, wanting it, enjoying the display of her body, welcoming the gaze of centuries of peeping toms as the elders find their counterparts everywhere. And the viewers of the paintings, admiring her nudity and the enticing stretch of her body, forget that this is a story of attempted rape, of a woman who could not speak in her own defence, who, but for the intervention of Daniel, faced death. The paintings make voyeurs of us all as we enjoy the sight that the elders stole from behind the bush, burning with lust and desire.

When they bumped into each other in the bushes, the elders confessed to each other their common passion and cooked up their plan. Susanna bathed without knowing they were crouching in the shrubbery. But then they burst out and told her that either she was to let them have their way with her or they would swear under oath (and these were judges!) that they had caught her in the act with a young lover and get her stoned to death. She turned them down and the next day her accusers were believed and she was led off to execution. On the way God heard her prayer (not before time!) and sent a young man called Daniel. He tricked these old sleaze-balls into confusing their own evidence and the crowd tossed them off the edge of the cliff. Presumably Susanna fell happily into the arms of her husband Joakim, though she might have wanted to know where he was while the trial was going on. The hero of the tale is meant to be Daniel, and the story a kind of footnote to his adventures with the lions. But the person at the centre of the story ought to be Susanna. She was a woman of integrity and courage, but those things have been poor protection against painters and the tradition. The scoundrels at the trial ordered her to be unveiled so that they might feast their eyes on her beauty. The painters and presenters of this story almost ever since have done the same. We are often too much like the voyeuristic elders, gazing at the surface of one another. And sometimes we feel like Susanna ourselves, raw, exposed, nude before a world that laughs, lusts, assesses, grades and describes us. And even if we raise our eyes pleading for mercy, unseen hands draw away the veils we need to conceal what is private.

I imagine Susanna as a woman in her thirties. She has children, she is wealthy, living in a foreign land with diplomatic status and privilege. Her husband is at the consulate. She has designer clothes, a style all her own and someone is thinking of naming a perfume after her. She has everything her parents ever dreamt of, though they would rather she lived somewhere in the Home Counties than in upmarket exile. Her husband adores her, when he has time. She is the perfect society wife and goes down well with all the local dignitaries. One evening, Susanna is invited to join some of her friends for a night out. She's not sure why, but she goes. Outside the consulate garden the air smells different and Susanna shivers in the unfamiliar world. They go to a bar in a distant corner of the city and drink and dance to rhythms she has not known before. She sees a young man in a mirror across the room and her gaze turns and stays awhile. She is intrigued; the shape of his head, the cut of his jacket, the way he holds a glass. She moves closer and they dance, she with eyes closed, saying little. They drive back to his apartment in her car and the night is sweet and warm with desire. In the early dawn she stirs and sees him dressed for labouring and leaving for work. Later she lets herself out and then remembers that she does not even know his name. She looks at the doorbell and underneath she reads his name written there: Daniel.

A sweet encounter perhaps, more full of tenderness than Susanna's meeting with the elders. But still an encounter based on a surface look with no one looking deep. Enough to skim the surface, enough to touch and admire, enough to see only what will arouse and awaken. A brief encounter, all reflected pain. Perhaps some of our relationships mirror this one. So many times we become voyeurs of one another, wanting to see all in another while keeping ourselves closed and safe. So many times we ourselves are frightened by the gaze of the world, of others who look only to criticize or lust or categorize. But true love will always involve going beyond the mirror, allowing ourselves no longer to be restricted to a reflective gaze, but to come into contact, to allow each other not merely a flat surface but breath and space and gesture. Susanna's story shows how strong is this human desire, to see others only on the surface and to keep ourselves from being seen at all. And yet, like all Susannas and all Daniels, we long for someone to see us as we truly are and still to love us and find us beautiful. Susanna was naked in the garden, being herself, singing gently on a warm afternoon. But to the elders she was nude, without clothes but not recognized for herself. She was something for them to look at, but never to know or understand. And no doubt she too, a rich woman with servants and privilege, was guilty sometimes of seeing only the surface of a person.

But Susanna knows how God sees. She knows that God sees her naked and not nude. At her trial she cries out to God, 'O eternal God, you know what is secret and are aware of all things' (Susanna, verse 42). She knows that God sees as the one who knows everything and still looks with mercy, compassion and love. Not as the elders looked on her, not as she might have looked at her servants, but the knowing love, the love that sees every breath and space and gesture. This is how God sees us. To be naked before God is to be revealed, but not to be put pitilessly on display.

The mirror is often the symbol of vanity, of all that is superficial, self-obsessed and full of false desire. The mirror is the symbol of our ability to turn each other into surfaces to be looked at, to be objects of desire. But the mirror can also be turned to good. As Christian people we are learning a new kind of looking. What else is theological reflection? We are learning that we are mirrors ourselves, mirrors of the image of God. By looking deep into God we will become changed into that image. And if we look deeply into one another we will see the image of God reflected and lovely. The human soul reflects the glory and beauty of God, and all else fades in comparison. So often we see only in a glass darkly. But one day we will see one another face to face, and even one day we shall know God with such intimacy. Susanna looks out from the many paintings of her story and pleads with us to see her, not the surface of paint nor the surface of flesh, but the interior mirror of God. There are many faces which equally deserve and need to be seen, and really seen, for what we are or have it in us to be; not surfaces, not sights to be viewed, not victims and not mirrors for another's ego, but ourselves, holy icons of God.

On the road to Emmaus (Luke 24), the poor befuddled disciples looked, but they did not see. It was only when the stranger broke the bread that they recognized who he really was. And then, in the moment of recognition, he vanished from their sight. Perhaps in life as in the text, moments of insight are rare and for much of life we cannot see. The mirrors are tainted, the glass dark. But by God's grace, the image of God may be seen in the mirror of our lives as we look to Jesus who is the light which enlightens every dark place and shines bright in the night of every suffering. With Susanna we cry to God, 'O Eternal God, you know what is secret.' God sees us as we are and loves us. Amen.

Prodigal daughter
Luke 15.11–32

I've been feeling increasingly militant lately, militant about some things I had concluded were safely accomplished. It's just that I've been to two services recently which were about the church being inclusive, but in both of which women were given not much more to do than make the tea and read the Bible. And, even though I know that the public proclamation of Scripture may be actually the most significant part of our worship, it didn't feel like that on *these* occasions. I was very glad, for example, to be part of a service to celebrate the Anglican–Methodist covenant and very glad to be welcomed to a service to celebrate that there are many Anglicans who want the Church to be inclusive of gay people, but I was sorry that in the rush to celebrate these kinds of inclusiveness, women seemed to have been forgotten. It somehow seems churlish and in bad taste to mention it, given the significance of those services. And I know that it's imposs-ible to do everything all the time, and that I am as much part of a racist and sexist church as anyone else, but I thought I'd say it anyway.

And then there's the parable of the Prodigal Son, which I often hear as you do, and read of it in books and hear of it in Bible studies and even see it in paintings as wonderful as Rembrandt's, which I would give a good deal to see one day if I can get to-gether the fare to St Petersburg. And of course it's wonderful and shows us, in a story to stir the heart, of how loving and forgiving is the heart of God. But, I'm feeling militant again because . . . well, simply because I am not a father or a brother and never will be and neither will some of you. And though it seems somehow churlish to mention this of such a classic and beautiful story I still want to ask, 'Where are the women?' The only ones mentioned are the immoral women upon whom the elder son imagines his younger brother to have spent his inheritance, so even they might only exist in his overactive imagination. I am not the first person to ask as I read this story whether these two sons had a mother, or even different mothers. And whether they had any sisters. In Rembrandt's famous painting there seem to be some women sitting in the shadows, but they do not emerge into the light in many reproductions of the picture. They are in the shadows, in the background, hidden away. And you might say that these are ridiculous questions to raise, that I'm trying to take the story too literally, as though this was a real family and not a literary construct. But I know many other stories of fathers and their children and they make me see this story differently, especially as I am looking for what this story does not say or does not want me to ask. I have read and heard other stories than this one and I cannot read it on its own. I have also read and I have heard stories like King Lear and even Cinderella, stories in which a father does have daughters. In these stories we learn of a father who, by all the standards of both fact and fiction, makes a serious misjudgement about his children. King Lear sets his daughters a test because he wants to know which of them loves him most. In a story full of misunderstandings and blindness he gets it so bitterly wrong. He blesses the daughters who are heartless and scheming, Goneril and Regan, but he curses Cordelia, who is really the one who loves him most. Though the truth is finally uncovered, the story is a tragic one because Cordelia dies. Before her death she says words to her father that might have been written for the elder son to say in the Gospel parable. 'You have begot me, bred me, lov'd me: I return those duties back as are right fit. Obey you, love you, honour you' (*King Lear*, Act I, Scene 1). The story of Cinderella, unlike King Lear, has a traditionally happy ending, because Cinderella finds someone else to love her in place of her cruel father. But in this story too we see a father who loves the wrong daughters and who cannot see when he, in turn, is truly loved.

These stories of fathers and their daughters might lead us to read the parable in a different way, perhaps to make us less trusting of the father in the parable, and less certain that he is an obvious candidate for a metaphor for God. And perhaps the truth is that we have heard this story too often anyway to be unsettled by it any more, to have any real sense of its scandal, and of the way it transgresses the expectations of any hearer, but hinting at the possibility that this father loves both his children: the boring and the glamorous, the older and the younger, the good and the wastrel. Perhaps we need to hear another story. What if there was a daughter whose father abused her terribly, in whatever way that fathers can abuse their daughters. She was taken into care, in a far distant place and looked after by kind people who gave her the warmest and most generous love, while he was sent to prison to be abused by other prisoners in his turn. She grew up and, with such tender love as she received, the wounds began if not to heal at least to mend a little. One day, years later, she left her adopted parents for a while and went to look for her father. When she found him he was sleeping in a night shelter, his only solace in the bottle, and he had aged beyond his years. He was astonished to find that she had searched for him and she told him that she wanted to be his daughter still if he would let her. And he wept with remorse and joy. Could it be true that the kingdom of God is as scandalous and as amazing a place as that?

You see how it makes a difference even to a story if you include the women, if you let another voice be heard. And just so, it makes a difference to the Church, to every community and to our understanding of the gospel. God may be a father who can love a profligate son, but God is also a daughter who can love a foolish father, and a parent who can love the child we all of us are. All of us who are lost may be found again, all who have been forgotten or unnamed find ourselves included within the love of God. Even if human institutions and movements fail us or forget us, God will embrace us and draw us in. This is the gospel. Amen.

Part 2

PREACHING THE CHRISTIAN YEAR

A woman uses the lectionary

In the popular BBC television series *The Vicar of Dibley*, Geraldine tells her congregation in her first sermon that they should not be afraid that everything will be changed because the vicar is a woman. She reassures them, for example, that the 'hymns' will not become 'hers'. The Archbishop of Canterbury, Rowan Williams, has recently been beguiled into saying reassuringly that no great revolutionary change has happened with the presence of more women in the ordained ministry of the Church of England. However, it is true to say both that radical changes do actually happen, for example when a woman preaches, and also that we can choose, as women preachers, deliberately to introduce change and to speak of faith in new ways. This is a particular challenge and comes powerfully to the fore on the days in the year when the lectionary is pressed to serve the church calendar, when the readings from Scripture are already given an interpretive frame by the context of 'the day'. On such days most preachers are prone to ask what they can possibly say that's new. Hasn't it all been said before? Here then is an opportunity to ask what difference it might make if the preacher is a woman, or more precisely, what it might mean to preach from a woman's experience and with a deliberate intention to speak in new ways. Once these questions are raised it is possible to see how the patriarchal bias of Scripture has often been intensified by the pressures of the calendar, but that this pressure can be resisted, and for good ends.

Many lectionaries and calendars have worked (even if not intentionally) to intensify the androcentric bias of the biblical texts. Some have sought to temper it. But none, as far as I know, have struggled to subvert it. Women (and men) find themselves asked to preach then on themes throughout the year that are ripe for a fresh look. Sometimes these themes are so familiar and well established that it becomes hard to question them and preachers fear to say something different. But equally, such themes often repay reappraisal, and the celebration of a festival can be powerfully renewed when we look at its message from a different place and in a new way.

It is not, I would argue, the case that women will naturally (or essentially) tend to read the Christian story in a particular way simply because they are born as women. But it is true that women experience the world in particular ways because they experience it from within a woman's body and within cultures that work to define and give meaning to women's bodies and experience. A woman's body and a woman's life are not value-free facts, but come to us with values ascribed to them by the cultures in which we live. The meanings attached to a woman's body will vary from one context to another, but there is no context in which it is value-free. Thus, finding (or making) knowledge and faith while embodied as a woman is always different from imagining that knowledge and faith are simply 'there'. To be embodied as a woman makes a difference to how you know and how you are known, how you experience life, and how you talk about faith. This applies to all women everywhere and it applies just as much to a woman who is a preacher.

So, as women begin to preach from their bodily experience and to use their experienced lives as a resource for preaching, it is not that having a woman's body will simply determine a style of preaching or theological content, but that the experience of living life as a woman, with a woman's body, can become a recognized and powerful place from which to speak, and a place of resourcefulness for new ways of understanding. The preacher may then address the lives of women (and of men) in a way that has not been done before. A woman who preaches determinedly 'like a woman' will be able to make the faith new by using metaphors, stories and themes drawn from the bodily experience of women and by allowing the text and the theme of the day to find a new context.

Preaching from a woman's life will also raise questions about authority and performance. In many churches, preaching has been defined in deeply patriarchal terms. The 'successful' preachers have often been identified as powerful orators with deep voices and a particular kind of authoritative presence. For many congregations and for many women it will seem impossible to preach except by adopting traditional styles. There will be strong feelings that it is not done 'properly' by a woman because the gender conventions are under strain. How can the congregation hear as authoritative the voice of a woman who is more like their daughter than their father? But, for a woman who is learning deliberately and self-consciously to preach 'like a woman', such straining of gender conventions may offer opportunities: both a power to be seized and a prevailing discourse to be changed. Wisdom is found in using this 'peculiar' place well, for the creation of new visions and for the opening of neglected wells of grace.

In Thomas Troeger's book *The Parable of Ten Preachers*, the author tells the story of a preaching class in which the participants were asked to recall their best memory of a sermon or preacher that had a positive impact on their life, to ask why this sermon was so effective and to discern what this was telling them about finding their own voice as a preacher for the next century. A woman in the class was the first to speak. Katherine remembered going to church at a very troubled time in her life, a time when she had not expected much more than a trip down a not very pleasant memory lane. She discovered that the preacher was a woman about her own age. The preacher spoke about the Word as the personification of Wisdom, a female expression of God. For the first time in her life she heard a sermon in which feminine pronouns were used to address God and tears welled up in her eyes. Troeger writes, 'It was as though she had returned to her childhood home to find a welcome she had not expected. No longer were the men the only center of attention. Her experience, her belief, her feelings counted as much as theirs' (Troeger, 1992, p. 17). Katherine's faith had been revived by the presence and speech of a woman preacher, a preacher whose words connected with her own experience. As she described to the class her experience of listening to this sermon, she could see that they did not understand. So she described how when she had entered the seminar room she had noted the brass plaque on the door commemorating the women who had refurbished it. But inside, the room had only portraits of past seminary students who were all young white men. Katherine told the class of her hope that the Church would renew itself by 'taking everything off the walls and starting again'. It is not only that women's voices need to be heard, but that their experience needs to be named and brought to bear on the Bible and the tradition.

Walter Burghardt is a celebrated preacher and a well-known writer on homiletics. His book *Preaching: The Art and the Craft* has been very influential. In one chapter of the book he includes an address he gave at a national symposium on preaching, with a response to it written by Elisabeth Schüssler Fiorenza. This remarkable debate illustrates powerfully the significance of drawing on the experience of women for preaching on the Christian year. In his own lecture, Burghardt advocates 'study impregnated with experience' as a powerful preparation for preaching. He declares that his preaching is least effective when he experiences nothing, that careful study is never enough on its own. He then describes the process he went through in preparing a sermon for Advent Sunday. He writes of how he read Shakespeare and Gerard Manley Hopkins, Tennessee Williams and John Henry Newman in an effort to think as broadly as possible about human experience. Then he thanks Schüssler Fiorenza for her 'insightful, persuasive and moving address' and includes it in his book. Schüssler Fiorenza says that she speaks for the 'woman in the pew', the silenced majority. She argues that the absence of women preachers has meant that the 'experience' of which Burghardt writes has actually only ever been male experience:

> For all practical purposes women of the past and of the present have not preached and are in many Christian churches still excluded from defining the role of proclamation in terms of their own experience . . . the danger exists that the homily will not articulate the experience of God as the rich and pluriform experience of God's people, but that the male preacher will articulate his own experience and will declare and proclaim his own particular experience as the experience of God par excellence. (Schüssler Fiorenza, in Burghardt, 1987, p. 70)

Schüssler Fiorenza encourages male preachers to be attentive to a wider range of human experience. In turning to Burghardt's sermon for Advent, she writes: 'I was surprised that he does not think of taking into account the experiences of pregnant women and their sense of self' (Schüssler Fiorenza, in Burghardt, 1987, p. 76). But what is even more significant is that she argues that justice will only come to the Church when a wider variety of voices are heard, when women can own and name their own experience. It is not so much that men need to be more aware of women's experience (though they do), but that women need to be able to attend to and to understand the significance of what it means to experience life from where they are, and to celebrate this as a source of truth.

Schüssler Fiorenza also suggests that listening to the voice of experience is not enough. For example she suggests that it would be helpful to study feminist analyses of 'motherhood' as culturally constructed and mediated and that interpreting the story of Mary's pregnancy requires reflection on women's experience today. But she is clear, above all else, that the experience of men must no longer be understood as the paradigm of all human experience. The experience of living in a woman's body demands to be named, interpreted and remade in the pulpit.

All preachers, of course, are usually people trying to make sense of their own lives and of the lives and experience of others. Any of us can be helped in this task by reading and listening to the stories that people tell or write about their lives, all sorts of people, both men and women. We can all look for God in the human stories that we find all around us. All life stories are interesting, and not just the obvious ones like Oscar Wilde or Judy Garland or C. S. Lewis. I am sure I am not alone in believing that every single human being with whom I have ever had a serious conversation has a fascinating story to tell. Iris Murdoch was once asked in a television interview why she filled her novels with such extraordinary people, so many eccentrics, so many people with dark secrets and mysteries, so many people with desires of which they are ashamed, so many people with extraordinary psyches and powerful imaginations. She simply replied that she did not believe she was writing about extraordinary people at all. She was just writing about people. She knew what must be true, that all people are utterly extraordinary. We some of us work hard to hide it, but it is what lies beneath which is fascinating and revealing. And it is in this extraordinariness of human life where God is made known.

The novelist and theologian Frederick Buechner, more than many, consciously uses the materials of his own life story as the beginnings of theological reflection. He has written a book called *The Sacred Journey: A Memoir of Early Days*. He begins the book with these stunning words:

> If God speaks to us at all in this world, if God speaks any-where, it is into our personal lives that he speaks. Someone we love dies, say. Some unforeseen act of kindness or cruelty touches the heart or makes the blood run cold. We fail a friend, or a friend fails us, and we are appalled at the capacity we have for estranging the very people in our lives we need the most. Or maybe nothing extraordinary happens at all – just one day following another, helter-skelter, in the manner of days. We sleep and dream. We wake. We work. We remember and forget. We have fun and are depressed. And into the thick of it, or out of the thick of it, at moments of even the most humdrum of our days, God speaks. (Buechner, 1982, pp. 1–2)

It may be a test of a good piece of writing, or reflection or preaching, that it enables all of us to connect with human experi-ences beyond our own, and that it gives us a sense of being related to human beings who, though they have very differ-ent experiences from ours, are nonetheless 'just like us'. Good preaching also connects us with our own experience in new ways, and with our experience of the God who made each of us and who speaks to us within the stuff of life, the 'once upon a time' of all our lives. For too long it has been the assumption of much preaching that human experience is male experience writ large, and often beautifully too. But we now see more clearly than we ever did that human experience comes already mediated through the cultures and ways of speaking and knowing that we inhabit, and that we cannot 'get away with' attending only to one kind of human experience as though it were normative. Women are now learning to draw without shame, and indeed with bravura, on their experience of being women and finding that such drawing will lead to new knowledge for the whole Church. This provides fertile ground for the preacher and it may mean that what is said through the Christian year, as the familiar stories are read, will be new and, more importantly, will bear new life.

The sermons in this section have all been preached on familiar themes and mostly on high days and holidays. I hope they suggest ways in which the determination to preach self-consciously from the experience of being in the world and the Church as a woman might allow familiar themes to sound a new note – sometimes a discordant one, sometimes a harmonious one and sometimes perhaps a sweeter one.

The first sermon comes from that time in the Christian year when the themes are all about waiting and hoping and being ready, the time within or just before Advent, the time when hope seems unbearably tense as we wait even for the waiting time to begin. The text is the strange parable of the wedding garment (Matthew 22.1–14). The sermon refuses to rest with the notion that Matthew has simply got in some sort of muddle with his traditions and presumes that the text, as it stands, says something important. So it wrestles with the human experience of preparing for weddings, drawing upon stories in which the experience is not what 'should happen'. A feminist might of course be extremely sceptical about the possibilities of a ritual associated with a patriarchal institution like marriage as a source of truth and declare such an occasion irredeemably marked by sexism! But whatever judgements we might make about the institution of marriage itself, themes of waiting, longing and (un)fulfilment are common in women's lives. This sermon celebrates the power of women to find joy and to celebrate it even while it is being thwarted. Many women's lives are deeply compromised in all kinds of ways, but many women also have deep wells of courage and joy which can nonetheless defy in the name of hope the forces that drag them down. The man in the story who has no wedding garment is cast in the sermon as an emblem of those

who would ask us to be 'more sensible' while many women
have learned that joy is found beyond reason, in the place where
we dare to sing and dance anyway and to cling to an outrageous
hope. The sermon uses a technique of playfulness, of drawing
out themes from the text and asking how these 'play out' in
women's experience. Many commentators will ask what a wedding traditionally symbolizes or represents, but will not ask first
what it might evoke in the context of human experience today.
The stories used here to do this task are drawn largely from
women's experience and, being so drawn, the text is interpreted
in a new way.

The second sermon, on Isaiah 61.1–7, is for a Sunday close
to Christmas and draws very directly and obviously from the
lived reality of many women's lives. It asks, very honestly, how
Christmas can be good news. But it does more than moan that
Christmas is busy and stressful. It uses the Christmas experience
to reveal how some theological themes can bring not only blessing, but also bane, and to challenge how such messages may be
heard by those already oppressed by many cares, and oppressed
in ways which are rarely named in church. The sermon then
uses this experience of an oppressive theology to reinterpret the
prophetic hope not as a challenge to yet more action on our
part, but as a comforting and empowering voice. There have been
many feminist theologians who have pointed out that Christian
admonitions against pride do little to address the position of
women who have often suffered from an overdose of humility or
even humiliation. Similarly, this sermon overturns the tendency
to make Advent sermons a call to action, when experience reveals
this is the last thing some need to hear.

The Christmas sermon, on Luke 1.46–55, is, appropriately
enough, strongly incarnational. But it draws upon a woman's
experience of the body, of being identified as of 'the body' rather
than 'the mind'. It is extraordinary that so much of the rhetoric
of Christmas prayers and hymns seems to suppose that flesh is
abhorrent and fallen, reinforcing the false theology which identifies women with weak, sinful flesh and men with the purer
realm of ideas and abstract truth. However, the other side of
the Christian story, indeed a core theme, is that flesh is holy

and inhabited by God and this theme refuses to be silenced and constantly re-emerges. Women's voices among others, preaching the Christmas gospel from their own experience, enable this to happen.

The sermon for the first Sunday in Lent draws on feminist biblical studies to support its refusal to 'blame the woman' and to see the story of Adam and Eve (Genesis 3.1–19) only through the eyes of the male theologian Augustine. It is astonishing how one particular reading of this story has so dominated Christian history and thinking. But a different way of reading the text coupled with themes drawn from a feminist protest about familiar ways of understanding human experience enable this Sunday to have a very different feel. Combined with the story of Jesus' wandering in the wilderness (Matthew 4.1–11) the story of Eden becomes a vehicle for understanding human life not as a falling from bliss into sin, but as a path towards maturity through difficult experience. It proves very difficult to dislodge familiar readings of both of these texts, but beginning from women's experience may prove one way to do it. In any case, neither of the two biblical stories need be regarded as having fixed and immutable meanings. When they are placed beside experience in new ways this Sunday of the year is transformed.

The Palm Sunday sermon draws on a text often placed with the story of Jesus' entry into Jerusalem (Mark 11.1–10), the story of David dancing before the Lord (2 Samuel 6.16–23). But its focus is not so much on him as on his wife, Michal, who refuses (or perhaps is unable) to dance. The sermon begins from a deliberate choice to focus on the woman in the story and upon her casting as the critic and cynic, but the sermon asks from whence her sorrow comes and imagines what it would mean for her unhappiness to be healed. So, the sermon celebrates the traditional joy of Palm Sunday, but also invites those who find it hard to embrace the kind of unrestrained joy symbolized by dancing.

The sermon for Maundy Thursday questions and turns around a familiar reading of the story of this day (John 13.1–20), a reading that celebrates service and humility. It begins from the experience of women who are often pressed into such humble service, reflects on the way in which a line is often crossed from humility to humiliation and asks what the gospel has to say. It ends with the promise that the Christian story speaks of one who washes our feet so that we can stand confident and sure, rather than abase ourselves in oppressed humility. It is a commonplace of human experience, and we certainly see it in the Church, that the most powerful declare themselves servants while obscuring their own power over others. This sermon refuses to let a story of the inversion of power be used in the service of those who would dominate and humiliate.

The Easter sermon, on John 20.1–18, questions and plays with what might traditionally be seen as a distinction between 'natural' and 'revealed' theology. It draws on the way in which Easter is celebrated and described as a spring festival, a feast of natality, to evoke the joy and promise of resurrection. This traditional dualism within theology has often mirrored the other dualisms common to Western culture, of which male/female is another. So the sermon, in deconstructing and undoing one traditional dualism, also undermines the other in order to bring forth something new.

The sermon for Ascension is a kind of protest sermon, a protest against some traditional, phallic readings of the Ascension story (Acts 1.1–11) as a 'hero rising' story. It refuses to read this feast as a celebration of the elevation of Jesus to hero status and reads it instead as a story which, by removing the hero Jesus from the scene, enables all of humankind to 'rise'. In many ways it is a very orthodox sermon, saying no more than many have said about this story, but using a critique of cultures that celebrate extraordinary men to reveal how the story of Ascension might be read, against that tradition, to inaugurate a new kind of world. It was written from a woman's experience of exclusion from and rebellion against that kind of culture.

The Pentecost sermon has a similar theme, and proclaims very forthrightly that the Holy Spirit is for all God's people and not for the elite. It works to reinforce the fulfilment of Joel's prophecy at Pentecost (Acts 2.1–21) by telling it alongside the much less familiar (and hilarious!) story of Moses and the elders (Numbers 11.24–30). Bringing a less-told story into the frame causes certain themes and notes to resonate more powerfully in the reading of the familiar story. In a Church that has often developed and sustained a hierarchy of spirituality, even while denying that it does so, the women who have often been placed in a lowly place may speak with a particular authority and from a particular experience on these themes.

The sermon for All Saints (on Ephesians 1.15–23) completes a trilogy of sermons which work to undo the recurring tendency of the Church to develop elites, hierarchies and heroes. It draws from women's history and experience to revive an understanding of the whole people of God as 'the saints'.

All preachers preach from their experience, whether they are aware of it or not. The life you have lived and are living affects the way you read, the way you think, and the way that you frame words to speak what you believe to be true. But it is possible to turn self-consciously and deliberately to your own experience, and to your considered reflection upon it, as a source for knowledge of God and as a tool for reading, reflection and preaching. Of course, your own experience is of limited value unless it is what enables you to connect with the experiences of others and to think wisely about stories, faith and the world. The pulpit is not a place to air your own life story for the sake of it or to work out in public your own traumas, fears and troubles. But used well, and sifted through careful thought and prayer, experience can be a rich mine for the preacher who wants to speak of human truth and the gospel. I am sure I have not always judged this well, but I am learning how my own embodied experience, the experience of a woman, may open up resources for preaching. The first step is to notice and to recognize that my own experience is particular and located, and that therefore I cannot automatically and easily speak for 'humankind', as many preachers in the past have assumed they could. The second step is to face my own experience as honestly as I can and to bring it with me, openly and consciously, as I read the Bible and prepare to speak to a congregation at significant times for all of us. The third step is to let the product of that encounter be formed in such a way that it can speak to those who have very different lives and experience from my own, and yet who long to know God as I do.

As a woman who preaches, and thus who is a key theological voice in the congregation, I have a particular challenge, because the voices of women are so newly heard in the Church. As the faith as we have received it engages deeply with the experiences of women's lives, it will be changed. And changed, not only for women, but for all God's people. That is the task for which, I would argue, women preachers are called.

Dressed for a wedding
Matthew 22.1–14

'Rejoice in the Lord always; again I will say, Rejoice.'
(Philippians 4.4)

There is a short story somewhere on my shelves about a wedding. It's a rather poignant story, poised in that space all too common in human life between sadness and joy. The wedding is beautiful, the banquet superb, the flowers divine, and the dress brings gasps of delight to all who see it. But in this story there is no groom. It's not just that he failed to turn up or got cold feet, but it turns out there never was a groom. The heroine of the story, the beautiful bride, has longed all her life for this wedding, from the day when she first put a lace curtain over her head as a child. But the right man has never appeared. So instead of waiting, she has decided to have a wedding anyway. There is a moment of embarrassment as the service does not actually take place, but the banquet continues and the bride is beautiful and happy. Reading the story, I wasn't sure whether I wanted to slap her or congratulate her. But whatever you think of her, she is the complete opposite of the poor wretch in Jesus' parable, the man who was not dressed for a wedding.

And I don't want you to think that I read nothing but wedding stories, but there's a beautiful novel by John Berger called simply *To the Wedding* which I have read many times, if only to relish the beauty of its prose. In this story there is both a bride and a groom and they are deeply in love. But the bride, unknown to the other guests, is not far from death. She is dying of AIDS. They travel to the most beautiful place in Italy to be married. There is warm sun, music, wine and dancing, and the people in the village square, unknowing of what it to come, wish them long life and joy. The bride asks the one she loves, 'What shall we do before eternity?' but she answers for him when she tells him that they will 'dance without shoes'. And so they dance together on the scrubbed boards of the tabletops, for joy, in defiance and in hope. These two, embracing joy, are also the complete reverse of the man in Jesus' parable.

But of course I am not really talking about weddings at all. I am talking about God's promise of joy in the midst of human life, of the foretaste of heaven in any dark day, of the hope that there is a different and more beautiful world threaded somewhere in the stuff of this one which at any moment might be revealed to us in the days of our lives. A wedding in the Bible is almost always more than a wedding. It is a sign, a sacrament of the new world that God is bringing, promising joy for everyone alive. Jesus spoke of himself as the bridegroom not because, as far as we know, he was ever married but because he brought good news and because he told even the most wretched among us that joy awaits us if we can only open our eyes and hearts to welcome it. He spoke often of weddings, feasts, banquets, brides and maids and dancing. And he spoke of these not because he was senti-mental or romantic, or because he thought marriage better than singleness, but because just as bread is a symbol of life, so a wedding banquet may be a symbol of love and of the heaven to come in which every loneliness is banished and every joy at last fulfilled.

It is tempting to think that the goal of a preacher is to make the Bible relevant to all our lives, to show how it speaks about the realities we already know. But of course the preacher is to do nothing of the sort. Because the Bible points to a reality we do not yet know, but for which we are invited to look, to hope and to wait. The Bible is given us because it can show us a different world, one strange to the one in which we struggle and labour each day, a world which may be closer than we know, but from which we so easily separate ourselves, a world which is both close at hand and far away, a world which Jesus longs to open for us and welcome us into. Just as my wedding stories challenge the emptiness and sadness we know so well, by defying them and dancing in spite of them, so Jesus breaks apart the regular world in which we live and invites us to a new one, a world in which joy is unbounded and love cannot be overwhelmed.

The parable of the wedding garment, it is true, is certainly a strange one. It looks as though even Matthew wasn't quite sure what to do with it. It comes tacked on rather clumsily at the end of the parable of the banquet, that story we all know well (though better from Luke 14.16–24) about the man who held a banquet and invited guests. They wouldn't come and sent their very worthy apologies, but the host didn't cancel the band and send the caterers home. Instead he invited anyone who could come, even good and bad alike. You don't have to be righteous, stylish or family to come to this party, it's open house. It's as though the Duke of Marlborough were to invite anyone at all to come to his son's wedding. Blenheim Park is filled with revellers and the palace is packed with guests. But in the strange parable added on at the end the king spots a guest who is not ready for the wedding, who is not wearing the right clothes, and when he can't explain why, he is thrown out on his ear with the promise of weeping and wailing and grinding of teeth. It seems a ridiculous end to the banquet story. If he was dragged in off the street at the last minute, how could he possibly have been expected to be wearing wedding clothes? There was no time for a trip to the shops or even to go home to change, so it seems very unreasonable indeed to expect him to have top hat and tails to hand! And, odd though Bible stories might be, we shouldn't expect them to be that odd. So what on earth shall we make of it?

Well, it looks as though Matthew was in a rush to meet the publisher's deadline for this chapter and so he's put two stories together that don't quite belong. And there's always going to be some careful armchair reader with plenty of time on their hands to spot that this was a bit of a botched job. We can probably make sense of this strange parable rather better if we cut it out and read it on its own. But of course, we should always read it on its own with lots of other things in mind!

Many of you will have planned weddings yourselves and I'm involved in one in two weeks' time, so weddings are much in my mind. And, despite the parable, I am saving myself the pangs about what to wear by being 'the minister' and opting for my usual Puritan black. But weddings in Jesus' time were a bit different from ours. There may have been less call for video cameras and cars, but there were plenty of other customs. When a couple got engaged or betrothed in his time the bridegroom kissed his intended farewell and said, 'I am going to prepare a place for you', words which might have a familiar echo. He had to go to his father and get things ready and he could only set the date for the wedding when his father agreed it. The bride had little to do but wait, knowing that the groom might come back at a moment's notice to claim her. She would keep her veil and a lamp beside her bed, so that she could be ready at any time. You might think it would be better to get a life, but I don't make the rules and that's how it was! And I hope that you might be remembering already some other things that Jesus said, and other stories he told, about bridesmaids and lamps, about foolishness and wisdom, and readiness. And if I tell you that among the stories of other teachers in Jesus' time are stories about a wedding banquet, and a fool who wasn't ready, you might get a sense of what the parable is about after all. It's not a story about dress codes and exclusion, as though the kingdom of God is like a gentlemen's club from which we might be thrown out for having no tie. It's not even like some of those churches in other cultures from this one from which you can be asked to leave for failing to have your shoulders properly veiled. It's not that the kingdom of God is policed by fashion fascists or style gurus, or even by angels who keep out the unrighteous or the unworthy. Perhaps we might not read the parable as a warning, but as an encouragement to live in a certain way, in a certain way of hope and the expectation of joy.

The guest who wasn't prepared was one who didn't think it worth waiting, who was living in a cynical state of realism, with no expectation that the feast would really happen. He was just the opposite of the people in my wedding stories who were so ready to celebrate, so eager to embrace joy, that they were dressed for a wedding when others would not have bothered. This guest, the one in the parable, has decided to stay in the workaday clothes of the ordinary world. He does not believe in the banquet. He is not ready. He cannot see that joy is around the corner. And so he finds himself in the midst of joy, in the world beyond the looking glass, in Narnia, in the kingdom of God, but the dust of earth is still upon his shoes and he is not prepared. I like to think that the parable could have a different end, that wedding clothes might be provided, even for those who have turned down every invitation or not even opened the envelope of life. But perhaps the parable warns us that we are in peril of missing the gift of life if we do not believe that it could ever come.

The wedding guest with the wrong clothes is like many of us who are ill-fitted for the great miracle of life. Or like any human being who cannot for a moment leave behind worries and problems to welcome the joy which waits to embrace any of us who will allow our hearts to race at the sight of one we love or sing an ode to joy with Beethoven or run with the wind down a green hill where the trees shake their branches in the wind. Perhaps the poor soul without the right clothes stands for all of us who sometimes miss the point about being a human being, that it's not enough just to sign the visitors' book, just to be here and half aware of what's going on around us. Life is something to be seized with both hands, something to weep with joy that we have received it, and to be lived out with relish and delight, whenever we can. We are strange creatures. God invites us to the feast of life, but sometimes we'd rather do something more worthy instead. We'd rather stay in our workaday clothes than put on the glad rags of the heart.

The Bible promises us that God invites us to the feast of life. And it encourages us to believe that human life is best lived on tiptoe of expectation, looking, waiting, and ready for the gifts of God. God wants you to enjoy the gift of life, never to refuse joy, and always to find in even the most burdensome day a space for love, for celebration and for that true holiness which is always on the verge of praise. Only as those who are ready for joy shall we be ready to embrace the new world that God is making, in which tears will be wiped away, and in which a true and deep peace will come. Amen.

Christmas as good news
Isaiah 61.1–7

In Allison Pearson's novel *I Don't Know How She Does It* there's
an opening scene which just about sums up something about
Christmas. A working mother is in the kitchen very early one
school day just before Christmas. She's roughing up some shop-
bought mince pies to make them look homemade so that she
isn't scorned by the other mothers when her children take them
to school. When I first read this scene I absolutely recognized the
pressure she is under, to be the perfect mother and to do her
job, to meet all the requirements of Christmas and somehow to
be able to snatch a few hours' sleep. I can't think of a better scene
to express the realities of many women's lives at this time of the
year. And, in some cases, men's too.

On a train journey recently, that novel came back to my mind
as I heard some of the conversation around me. I was sharing
space with two working mothers who were telling stories about
how they are coping with Christmas. One of them, with three
small children, has refused to go away this year, so all the family
are coming to her, all eight of them. The other told the story of
how her children were going to a Christmas craft party that night,
and she wearily said, 'Aren't some mothers amazing!', knowing
just how much someone's mother would have done to organize
that. They were both going to have to do all their Christmas
shopping in one day and they were exchanging notes about the
best ways to order food over the internet for all those house
guests for all those days, and how to make sure they would have
the immense number of yoghurts and loo rolls and milk cartons
that everyone would need. All of this was interspersed between
work phone calls and reading the papers for the next meeting

and stories about work rotas and the merits of full-time or part-time work. When we all got out at Paddington I inwardly wished them well and hoped that somewhere in the midst of all of this, they would get some time for themselves, and I hoped that someone would buy them a nice present.

I've enjoyed watching the TV programme *Grumpy Old Women at Christmas*, in which women about my age moan about all the stuff you have to do and remember and organize and cope with over the Christmas season. Aren't women wonderful! But Christmas *is* a huge pressure for some people. Even if you have very modest plans, it's not easy to be responsible for Christmas. There's so much to do, there are so many expectations, and it's exhausting. And of course there are other things too that make Christmas demanding. If, at the same time as Christmas is going on all around you, you're feeling lonely, or if Christmas brings sad memories, or if it suddenly makes you more aware than ever that your life is not what you wanted it to be, then it's hard. I do love Christmas, but I see more and more that for many people it doesn't bring straightforward joy.

But you might think that it's better for people who are Christian, of course, because we understand *the real meaning of Christmas*, and all that prayer makes for a Zen-like calm spirit which will carry us through the Christmas rush with our blood pressure completely normal and our hearts full of good will. Well, I don't think so. Christians are by no means immune from the rush and the pressure and the anxiety that the myth of the perfect Christmas represents. And I sometimes think that Christians are under even more pressure than most people at Christmas. It's not just that we've got all the Christmas services to go to (or in some cases organize!), it's not just that we have extra things to do like carol singing, decorating the church as well as home, or working out what to buy the minister for Christmas. There's something else. Christmas brings a whole new wave of guilt.

For a start, there's the strong feeling that Christmas is too much about consumerism and material things. The amount of money we all spend in December is probably scandalous, and we feel bad about it, but of course we don't stop doing it. You can quell some of the guilt by buying fairly traded chocolate or gifts from Oxfam Unwrapped, but it won't ever quite go away. And if you complain about all the spending and the buying, the extravagance and the luxury, then you end up feeling like Scrooge, and then of course you can feel guilty about that.

And then at Christmas in church you get readings like the one we heard from Isaiah today:

> he has sent me to bring good news to the oppressed,
> to bind up the broken-hearted,
> to proclaim liberty to the captives
> and release to the prisoners.
>
> (Isaiah 61.1–2)

There's a Christmas carol with a chorus that speeds up, and we sing about how God has sent us to bring the good news to the poor, tell prisoners that they are prisoners no more . . . And we think, or I think, and maybe you think, 'Yes, I know, I should be doing more for the oppressed. I should have gone to London to campaign to MakePovertyHistory instead of going Christmas shopping. I know, I should spend less on Christmas and give more to the poor. And, I know, I know, I should spend more time giving hospitality to the lonely and comforting the sad. As well as getting Christmas organized, I should be doing more . . . And I feel guilty about that, and maybe I even begin to resent Christmas for making me feel so wretchedly guilty about all the things I haven't done.'

But then, maybe, if you can find a prophet who will sit you down, make you a good cup of fairly traded tea and tell you just to pause for a moment, you will listen to that passage again. Because the prophet doesn't say that you have to do those things at all. The prophet doesn't say that this is your agenda, it's not yet another Christmas list that you have to pick up. These tasks are not, in the first place, for you, and certainly not for you alone. These words are read at Christmas because Jesus, the one whose coming we celebrate now, once quoted them and took them for his own. And perhaps you'd better listen to the story of his life and hear how he made all this the centre of his life. And then, if it's not so much that this is another list of tasks for you to do, another list of impossible and unachievable goals, perhaps it's something quite different. Perhaps it says that God's gift to you is that somewhere out there in the great universe is a God who wants to bring YOU some good news. Just for once, stop feeling responsible for the whole world, stop cursing the darkness and shaking your fist at the stars and at God and at Delia Smith and all those who want you to save the world single-handed, including yourself – and hear the promises of God.

The prophet comes to bring good news to the oppressed, those oppressed by life in this bit of the world every bit as much as those oppressed by things we can barely imagine. We are rich in things, but often poor in soul, oppressed by the powerful culture of consumerism whose temptations are hard to resist. God offers us good news here too, the still, small voice in the shopping centre, the presence of the Christ-child in the midst of our noise and anxiety as much as in the midst of a Roman census. The prophet promises that God will bind up the broken-hearted, hold together those who are falling apart. There is good news for us too; for the depressed and the addicted, for the harassed and those screaming or weeping into their pillow at night. The prophet promises freedom to the captives, and that promise is for us too, in whatever captivity holds us. God comes to set us free, from worry and the restless search for meaning in a world empty of hope. From any and every one of our chains, God comes to set us free. And the prophet says that God comes to comfort those who mourn, to comfort us in every loss of someone close, of the hopes we once had, of the sorrows that make our hearts ache. The promise is for us, as it is for all God's people.

It's so easy for Christmas to become law and not gospel, work and not grace. How can we find spaces within the days of Christmas to receive this grace of God, and to welcome Christ among us? How can we find the place, the silent, peaceful place, where Christ can come to heal us, to set us free, to bind our wounds and to comfort our sorrows? Only so will we find the place of our birth, when we will find a new life in the brokenness of our own times.

I shall try not to be a grumpy old woman this Christmas! But I shall also give up trying quite so hard, and give God just a chance to transform all that my life is. I hope that in the spaces of our celebrations, and even in the very midst of them, Christ will come and make us all new, set us free, hold us together and bring us good news. For this is the gospel. Amen.

Body and blood
Luke 1.46–55

Today, at a communion service, the talk is of body and blood. The body and blood of Christ, given and poured out for us, and the body and blood of Mary, giving birth in a stable to a baby who was God with us. There is talk of dying and of being born.

In every congregation I have known there have been those who have had difficulties with the communion service, even to the extent of staying away or leaving after the sermon. Some have told me that they find the idea of body and blood revolting. What are we doing, eating the flesh and drinking the blood of Jesus? Isn't this just a disgusting relic of ancient and primitive cultures?

These honest questions are getting at something serious. But maybe, in order to answer them, we have to start from a different place. The legend goes that one of the women theologians of the Reformation, Jane Grey, the nine-days' queen, had some comments to make to those who accused her of heresy. When they said to her, 'Did not Our Lord say "this is my body", "this is my blood"?', she replied, 'He also said, "I am the vine", "I am the door", but was he a vine, was he a door?' Of course he was not literally a door or a vine, and neither, one might say, was the bread literally his body or the wine his blood. This is all a kind of category mistake. But how else could we understand it all?

Many of the Hebrew prophets went in for prophetic signs. Jeremiah once took a clay jar and broke it in pieces in the very place where human sacrifices were going on (Jeremiah 19.10). This was the tradition that Jesus lived and breathed. Prophets did not only speak, they acted. Like all good teachers they were good at show as well as tell. And Jesus had his own prophetic signs. On that night, the last night on which he was to share a meal with his disciples, he took the bread and broke it and said, 'This is my body, which is for you.' And then later, when the meal was over, he took the cup and said, 'This is my blood, the blood of the covenant, shed for many.' He was telling them what was going to happen to him and telling them what it meant. They did not know as we do now that he was going to die. They did not know that his death would be somehow redemptive, that it would bring about a new understanding of the relationship between God and God's people. They knew none of this. He was telling them he was going to die, that this was his last meal. Perhaps he had been trying to tell them what was bound to happen for a long time. Perhaps they were unwilling to believe it. So Jesus had to show them in this brutally clear way. You see this bread, this is my body, this is what will happen to me – and he breaks it. You see this wine, red like blood, poured out, this is what will happen to me on the way to the kingdom of God.

You will think perhaps that I read of this approach to the Last Supper in some scholarly book or that I learned it sitting at the feet of someone great. I didn't, though perhaps I could have done if I had listened hard enough. It came to me as I stood presiding at communion for the last time in my first pastorate. I stood behind the table barely able to reach the plates and chalices because I was heavily pregnant, about eight months gone. As I said the words 'This is my body' and 'This is my blood' given for you, I was suddenly intensely aware of several things. I knew that my body was being given and would soon be given in a dramatic way, to the giving of birth to another. I knew that I was afraid, of the pain and the danger and all the things that could go wrong, of the unknown, of becoming a parent, of the blood and of my own body. I also knew, looking out over some of the dear people of my first pastorate, how much I had given of my body, my self, my lifeblood, to them over the past three years and I felt weary and worn, but intensely glad to have given what I could. And I was also aware of the distant but powerful echo of Jesus on that night of all nights when he stood before those whom he loved and showed them by tearing bread and pouring wine what was soon to happen to him. This was a powerful and dramatic sign of what awaited him. Maybe he recognized as he never had before, what his commitment to God was going to cost. And maybe he recognized too that it was worth it. If the cause is right, if the love in your heart is strong enough, it is worth offering yourself, body and soul, to the point of breaking and bleeding, so that life may be made new.

Mary was, according to Luke, able to rejoice in her pregnancy and to see it as the favour of God. And she spoke the words of a prophet, telling of how God changes the world, raising high the lowly, filling the hungry with good things. And her sign, the prophetic sign of Mary the prophet, was her body, the growing belly, her stretch marks and her swollen ankles, all signs that God was about to be born, to be embodied, made flesh, among us and for us.

And there is Jesus' body, the first angry cries in the draughty stable, the first desperate sucks, the first gentle snuffles, God gracing flesh, becoming just like us. And we remember how, when grown and strong, he broke bread and poured wine, as a promise that he would give his body for us. Like a mother, he struggled for us with his own body, bleeding and gasping, so that we and all creation could be born again, dying to all that defeats us and rising to all that makes life good and beautiful and filled with love. God abhorred not the body of birthing nor the body of dying. God loved being some *body*, loved all the delights of the body and accepted its pains and frustrations, but was ultimately willing to suffer its agony and death, so that new life could be born. He showed his disciples this as they ate bread together and shared the cup of wine.

And then there are our bodies. Our faith, a faith which celebrates that God became flesh, should show us that bodies are places of God's presence and joy, whatever shape they are, however wounded they are, however much pain they feel or joy they desire. Our faith, a faith that has this holy meal at its heart, also shows us that our bodies are a gift we can give to others, for love, for friendship, for service in all kinds of ways. As Christ gave his body and his blood for the kingdom of God, so he invites us to give ourselves, body, mind and soul and strength to God. And as he was raised to new life, so we too are offered new life in him.

This communion service is not a bizarre kind of cannibalism. But it is about bodies and bodiliness, about God becoming flesh in Mary and in Jesus and in us. It is about Jesus giving his body to die for us so that we could be born. It is about our bodies, about what cause we shall give them to, what we would die for and what we live for. At Christmas we remember that God became some *body*, that we who are also somebody are invited to become one with Christ. Mary said, 'My soul tells out the greatness of the Lord,' but it was with her body that she did it, and we are invited to tell out God's glory with our bodies and souls, to the glory of God. Amen.

First Sunday in Lent
Genesis 3.1–19; Matthew 4.1–11

The process of growing up is a profoundly uneasy one, and it seems to take longer than you first think. One of the effects of my father's death has been to leave me feeling that I have to grow up, and in a way that I'm instinctively reluctant to do. My father is no longer here and I must get along without him. I am propelled into a bleak and empty space and I must navigate my way through it. This kind of growing up is part of life and everyone has to face it in some way or another. We are made so that part of our life is the process of maturing, flourishing, and coming of age. And if life goes as it should then the wilderness times and the growing times are very important indeed. Jesus, it is true, used to take a child and place the child in the midst of the crowd and say that this is what it means to enter the Kingdom. But whatever it was that he meant by that, it wasn't I think that we should remain childish and avoid the paths of maturing and growth that lie before us. Those looking on at religion and at religious people have often accused us of being infantile, of clinging on to childish stories and dreams, as though reading the Bible were like reading fairy tales. And they are right to criticize us when religion is used in that way. But lived rightly, faith in God is a path to maturity, to spiritual adulthood or wisdom. It is not for nothing that the early Christians spoke of the Christian life as being about growth into the full stature of the maturity of Christ. Faith is a form of growing up, not of childish avoidance.

In the story of Jesus in the wilderness, I think we see a story of someone growing up and coming to terms with who he is and who he will be. We see someone tempted by immaturity, tempted to take the easy way of instant gratification, the stones into bread. We see someone tempted by fame, power and spectacle, the kingdoms of the world and the dramatic rescue by angels. But in the end we see someone choosing the mature path of faithfulness to God's word and trust in the God who is with us in the ordinary world we must inhabit. Here is someone who has journeyed through the wilderness for a long stretch of time and who has grown into the one who will carry God's presence into the world. We have learned to read this story as a story about the temptation to sin and used it to reflect on the temptations that present themselves to us in our very different world. But today I offer a reading of this story as a story of growing up, of facing the wilderness that we must all inhabit and of living a mature and responsible life within it.

I suspect that the story read like that draws on another story, the story of Adam and Eve. Their story begins not in the wilderness, but in a garden, but they, like Jesus after them, have to learn to live in the wilder and more dangerous place. They too have to grow up, and perhaps this was God's plan all along.

Most of us in the Church have grown up believing that the story of Adam and Eve and the snake has a clear meaning, that it is about Original Sin and The Fall. This must go down as Augustine's greatest triumph, that sixteen centuries after him we are still inclined to regard his interpretation of this story as the natural one and the only good one. It's so dominant that we hardly recognize it is even an interpretation, it's just what the story is about. But it wasn't until about a thousand years after the story was first written down that Augustine read it his way, and many previous readers of this text would have thought his interpretation very odd. He read the story through what Paul said about Christ being the second Adam. He believed that sin came into the world through Adam and Eve, that it was passed on through sexual desire, and that Christ was the one who undid all this by dying for us. Augustine's reading has a good deal to say to us about the inescapability of sin and the grace of God revealed to us in Christ. But it is not the only way, and certainly not the most ancient way, of reading the story of Adam and Eve. There is another way of understanding this story which has its roots in the Jewish community and which is based on a close and attentive reading of the text itself. In this reading, the story is not so much about sin, temptation and fall, as it is about the maturing of human beings and about their relationship with the rest of creation. And I have learned this reading from a Dutch Old Testament scholar called Ellen van Wolde.

In the beginning of Genesis chapter 2, the Bible describes the earth in its early days as being without anyone to till it, to cultivate it. But then God makes a human being from the earth itself. 'Adam' means really something like 'earth creature' and is not a man's name, but simply the name of an earthling. This creature is then placed into a garden, where he/she must till it and keep it. The text here talks much more about the earth and the ground than about the human being, but of course we, being human beings, always take more notice of the bits about us. And this earthling is like a child, living in paradise, knowing nothing of good and evil, and not even knowing of death. This is a creature ignorant, naive and protected. Then God notices that the human being is alone, and so God separates the creature into two, into male and female. But then the human beings, encouraged by the snake, lose their innocence. They eat of the tree of the knowledge of good and evil. They become sexually mature and aware. And they discover that life must be hard work, that some human beings will dominate others, that there is suffering to be borne. And they discover the reality of death. The human beings leave the garden. They leave the innocent world of their childhood and are pushed into the wilder world of grown-up human living. And now, at last, the earth has someone to cultivate it and make it fruitful. The creatures made from earth have work to do on the earth and they must get on with it. In the story, it is necessary for the good of the earth that there are creatures to cultivate it so that it can bring forth plants, and so this is a positive development for the earth even if for the human beings it seems a descent from paradise. As far as the story is concerned the human beings are bound to the earth, by their very name, by their origin. These grown-up human beings are those who complete the creation story by working to make the earth fruitful. If this reading is right, then it is not that Adam and Eve 'fell' away from God's original intention for them, but that they had to find maturity and their true purpose within creation. They (we) were not made for idleness in paradise, innocent of good and evil, like perpetual children, but were always intended to grow up and to live in the harder, but more adult world. This coming to maturity is exemplified in the Adam and Eve story by their coming to sexual maturity; they know they are naked, they can have children, by their gaining of the knowledge of good and evil, and by their experience of the reality of death. These are the markers of human maturity, of what God intends for us. This is not punishment for some 'original sin', but simply what it means to be human. Children in paradise, knowing nothing, making no moral decisions and thinking themselves immortal are not yet mature human beings. And God has, in this story, and in all our lives, made it possible for us to learn what it is to be human and to know this as God's will for us. The story of Adam and Eve is a kind of parable of the process of human growing up, and thus it is the story of all of us. If our lives are to bear good fruit we have to grow up and mature, and though this has a cost for us it is what we are called, propelled, led to do. If we are to 'come of age' we have to learn that life is more like the wilderness than the garden, that we will have to make judgements and decisions, that life will bring pain and that it will end. But we also learn that only in this life, and not in a protected paradise, may we become fully human, bearing the image of God, and grow into the maturity of the stature of Christ.

There are those in the Jewish tradition who have always seen this story as being about the growing up of human beings. So perhaps for today at least we should try to shut out other readings and listen to theirs. I am committed to a path of religion that is about human flourishing and maturity and not about keeping people in a childlike naivety. Christians, you might say, should be more 'knowing', more mature, more worldly-wise than anyone else. Christians, you might say, should be more strongly committed to engaging with the world as it is than anyone else. We know what the deal is and we have resources to get on with it, to live in the wilderness and to face down those who would tempt us to escape from it or live in denial of it. And we are those who know that ignorance is not bliss after all, that there is a deeper joy to be found in facing the world as it is, and that God is with us, even and perhaps especially when the way is hard.

As we begin the time of Lent, we read the story of Jesus in the wilderness. He, like Adam and Eve, had a tempter, but this tempter tried to lure him back to the innocence of the garden, to a place where nothing had to be worked for, but only asked for, a place where he could be protected from death by angels, a place where the whole world could be his for the asking. Jesus, of course, rejected these temptations and stayed resolutely in the wilderness as it truly was: a place of hunger, a place of emptiness, but a place where God is and where God can be worshipped. And he shows us how to live in this place too, in whatever form it comes to us. There are no childish promises of escape, but there is an example of a mature human life, and the promise that God is with us.

At times, in all our lives, we are propelled against our will into a place where we must grow up before God. These are not easy times, but they bring us gifts too, gifts which we are foolish to refuse. May this Lent be a time for the maturing of life and faith among us, as we grow into the full maturity of the stature of Christ. Amen.

Palm Sunday
2 Samuel 6.16–23; Mark 11.1–10

David said 'I have danced before the Lord.' (2 Samuel 6.21)

When David danced with abandon before the Lord, his wife disapproved and told him off. She said it was vulgar and that the servants would laugh. But David told her he would go on doing it anyway. He had brought the Ark of the Covenant, the presence of God, to the city of Jerusalem. The holiest and most precious symbol of the faith of Israel had entered the city at last. For David that was cause for dancing and celebration. And centuries later Jesus was carried into the city of his ancestor David, Jesus, the one in whom the poor and the sick, the sinners and the desperate saw at last the holy presence of God, and the crowds shouted Hosanna and called him the Son of David and were as abandoned with joy as David had been when he danced before the ark of the Lord. But you don't have to read many verses before you find the word 'indignant', and find that there were those who tried to silence the children shouting Hosanna and who thought the wonderful things Jesus was doing were vulgar and blasphemous. Has it always been so, that good people refuse joy and cannot let themselves dance before the Lord?

A while ago someone pointed out to me what a strange title the Church of Scotland magazine has: *Life and Work* – not *Life and Joy* or *Dance and Sing* but something much more earnest. And 'Reform' of course is not so different. Revolution might be more to the point! How is it that religion so easily turns from joy to something more earnest? Well, perhaps because we need to work hard to survive and live, because without serious thought we will go astray. But sometimes, sometimes, and perhaps more often than we think, we are called to dance before the Lord, to know joy and delight and to find bliss before God and with each other. The story of Palm Sunday is a kind of break-out moment. We all know what's going to happen, and Jesus must have known that his provocative entry into the city would lead to profound and dangerous trouble. But how could he keep from singing and dancing, and how could the crowds keep from celebrating, that he was with them and that they were in the holy city and that God was very close?

One of the things that often moves white, Western visitors to Africa, or to a black majority church here or anywhere, is the persistence of joy, of the powerful reality of song and dance, even and especially among people who have great cause sometimes to sorrow. Those communities reveal that joy is not the reverse of suffering, but a profound response to it, a refusal to be done down, a defiance of what seems to be the case, a refusal to be bound, and an affirmation of the reality of God even in the bleakest times. Again and again I have heard people come back from communities like these and speak of the deep faith and joy that refuses to lie down. Like David, they will say, 'I have danced before the Lord.' All worship arises from joy, but a joy that is forged in suffering and truth, and never in denial and whistling in the dark. It was said of the poet Christopher Smart that he knew that sink or swim, he must praise always, somehow or other. And someone told me once that he believes in coming to church because even if we cannot change everything about the world, we can at least always 'praise God' and that this will help us to continue on the way. The most perceptive of the disciples on Palm Sunday might well have known what the week ahead might bring them, but they praised God anyway, because God is to be praised. 'Before the Lord I shall dance for joy.'

But what of those who refuse joy or despise it or are discomforted by it? What of us, who are sober-suits for much of the time, born of a culture marked by restraint and formality? Let's listen to Michal's story to see if there is anything there to help us. We have read today only part of her story, the part where she seems a shrewish and peevish wife, telling her husband off for displaying himself in his underwear before the servants, making an exhibition of himself in a holy procession. Her words are

sarcastic and she sounds hard and bitter. And yet there is more
to say. Earlier in her story we have heard how much she loved
David, the only time the Bible ever tells us of a woman's love for
a man. The other story we know of her is the time she rescued
David from danger by letting him escape through a window. This
was a man she loved and longed to protect. But Michal was also
Saul's daughter, the daughter of the king that David usurped. She
is the victim of political events in which her father and husband
are rivals. And David's triumphant entry into the city is also a
defeat for her father. In the story, she watches from a window.
This is the classic place for a woman in so many ancient stories,
watching from the window, not participating, but only watching from a hidden place. Poor Michal cannot share David's joy,
because she is imprisoned by circumstances. She cannot dance.
And in the story of Jesus there were many who could not dance
with the disciples and who turned instead to criticize them and
him. The Gospel writer tells us that there were those who saw
the wonderful things Jesus was doing and who heard the children praising God with joy, but who could not celebrate, and
were indignant instead. These were the Temple officials, those
with an interest in a different system of salvation, with sacrifices
and offerings, and an institution and rules. Perhaps the very
need to preserve these things had closed their hearts to joy. But
if this were so, then we cannot be hard on them, for we know
this temptation too and we know the frustrations of a life in which
there is so much to do, so much important work and so much
that we cannot lay aside.

But David said, 'I have danced before the Lord.' David was not
a high scorer on morality and goodness. He was a warrior, an
adulterer, an assassin. He was not always happy either. He knew
great sorrow. But David knew how to dance before the Lord. If
only he could have found a way to invite Michal to join him, to
share with her the joy of the knowledge of God.

In one of the catechisms to which our tradition looks back,
to the question 'What is the chief end of man?' (*sic*!) comes
back the answer, 'To glorify God and to enjoy him forever.' The
Reformers would argue that joy is the gift of God and the purpose of human life. And they would agree with the Catholic

writer Evelyn Waugh, who believed that the refusal of joy is as much a sin as the neglect of duty.

We are made to enjoy God and to glorify God forever, to dance with delight that God loves us and finds us beautiful, to be glad that we are alive, and that God is good. The religious life, the life of every lover of God, is not a duty to be carried, a task to be done, a hair shirt to be worn scratchy against the skin. It is a source of joy, deeper than any sorrow can touch and more enduring than any pain. This profound joy can make even the concentration camp or the hospice or the loneliness of the darkest night of the soul once again warm with light and meaning. The presence of God can set prisoners dancing, allow even the deeply depressed an intimation of glory, can make even the condemned man sing God's praise. There are some sorrows that no struggle will erase, no duty will solve, no work heal. But even these cannot stamp out the possibility of joy. Many of us find it hard to abandon ourselves to joy. But I am repeatedly struck that it is those who have suffered worst who know how to seize joy with both hands and to relish this true gift of God. We should never refuse joy, never refuse to dance.

Imagine how the stories might be different, the story of Michal, the story of the temple officials and the chief priests, the stories of our own lives. Imagine Michal, set free to climb down from her window and join in the dance. She lifts the veil of disapproval, she hitches up her skirts and lets her body sway at last to the rhythm of the music. Imagine the chief priests setting aside their dignity for once, joining in the Palm Sunday procession, smiling broadly and singing Hosanna, holding hands with the children and dancing through the streets. And imagine yourself, whatever the reality of your life right now, finding again the possibility of joy. David said, 'I have danced before the Lord.' Let us, in whatever is our sweet style, find a way to join him, the disciples and all God's joyful children, in praising God, this day and all our days. Amen.

Maundy Thursday
John 13.1–20

A few years ago, on holiday in Greece, I was in a church dedicated to St Dionysius. I watched in silent horror as a woman about my own age came into the church and then crawled on her hands and knees from the door to the altar, an altar that bore the reliquary containing his bones. She did it so very matter of factly, in her flowered cotton summer dress and sandals. But it made my stomach churn to see a woman on her knees like that. I did not think any good could come of it.

There is in Rome a statue of St Peter. And the toes of the statue have been worn away by the kisses of thousands and thousands of adoring pilgrims. Over the generations many have worn away the feet with their adoration. But the thought of this somehow fills me with horror.

Once I was worshipping in a theological college when the great Archbishop Michael Ramsey was to be guest preacher. I was astonished, and rather caught off guard, to find that as he walked down the aisle at the beginning of the service, everyone knelt down as he approached. I found myself the only one left standing, because I did not feel I should bow or kneel before another human being, and certainly not in church, though I fear that my Protestant protest probably just looked like crass rudeness, as I suppose partly it was. I felt a bit the same when a member of the royal family came to visit my school, and I could manage only the most perfunctory of curtseys. It stirs something deep in me when I see one human being kneeling at the feet of another, especially if it is a woman to a man, or a black person to a white person. So how then am I to understand Jesus' instruction, 'You also ought to wash one another's feet' (John 13.14)? Do I need a good dose of humility? Well, in some ways probably I do. But I think the story as the Gospel tells it actually speaks directly to my dilemma.

The story we all might have expected to read is the story that would fit with all the stories I have told, the humble disciple bowing before the greater Lord, the ordinary mortal washing the feet of the remarkable saint, the penitent betrayer on his knees before a mighty Saviour. That story would fit with all our experience of the way things work. The lowly wash the feet of the great, the slave of the master. And that's the story that I dislike so much, the one I rebel against and protest against, the story that makes masters of some and slaves of others, the story that still has its power in our world today. But of course, that's *not* the Gospel story at all. In this story it is Jesus who washes the feet of the disciples, it is Jesus who takes the towel to the grubby feet of his friend Peter. This is not the mighty getting their due. It is instead the turning inside-out of the way of the world, the way it's always been. Peter tries to get the story back on track, to make it fit. 'You will never wash my feet!' (John 13.8). But Jesus insists that this is the way it's got to be. And that's how it is. The God he has come to proclaim and to embody does not expect or demand that we get down on our knees, or that we kiss the feet of his statue, or that we bow in dutiful reverence like slaves. This one has come not to be served, but to serve. He hasn't come to bolster up the status quo or to keep anyone in his or her place. He has come to offer everyone a new place in a new scheme of things.

Later on in the same long discourse in the Gospel, Jesus tells the disciples that he will not call them servants, but friends. The new community of the Church is to be a community of equals, a community of friendship. And, most significant of all, he does not tell them to wash his feet, but to wash each other's, not to love him even, but to love each other. Jesus proclaims the God who longs to love us as friends, and not to recruit us as slaves, the God who wants us to befriend each other rather than 'lord it' over each other. A song from Sunday school urged me to 'trust and obey', but I have learned that God asks not for my obedience, but invites and encourages my love and asks me to love others. And in Jesus I see God reaching out in friendship to the world. Knowing God is not about obeying a dictator or a King. It is the amazing discovery that the God who puts water in the desert and stars in the sky is friendly, and counts you as a friend. Jesus came to tell us that we are no longer to think of ourselves as the servants of the Gods, their playthings or their slaves. But we are God's friends, made and spun from God's love. And, as such, we are to be friends to each other.

It is striking in this story that Jesus does not ask the disciples to respond to his loving action by washing *his* feet. He asks them to respond by washing each other's. Could we take this to mean that Jesus came to tell us that God does not want us to spend all our time on our knees before him, but more of it on our knees before each other? Is this the echo of the God who told the prophets of old that he cared little for the sacrifices at the altars and the ceremonies of the religious? Is this the God who said that it was justice and mercy that count, love of God and neighbour above all? I think it is. Jesus stands in the line of all those prophets who called the people back to the ways of God. Human beings have this knack of slipping back into predictable and familiar ways. We like to know our place in the world. We like to know that, if there is someone before whom we must bow, someone above us on the ladder of life, well at least that means that there is someone below who will bow to us. We like to know that everything is in its place. We have our prayers to say and our duty to do. But Jesus came to throw everything into confusion, to overthrow proper order and show us a different world, a world in which masters kneel before slaves and in which even God comes to be human and to wash the feet of the poor.

Tonight, on what we have come to call Maundy Thursday, we are shown with astonishing clarity, the heart of the gospel. And it seems so different from the ways of the world or even the ways that the Church has learned and still, largely, lives by. Jesus asks us, not to kiss his feet, but to wash each other's feet, not to be servants of a greater God, but to be friends with God, not to give all our energy in religious practices, but to serve God by serving each other. In the world according to Jesus Christ, the way to worship God is to wash the grubby, smelly feet of a homeless man and to do it not as an act of virtue, but as an act of love. The way to worship God is not to close your eyes all the time in prayer, but to open your eyes to the faces of those all around you. It is not to crawl on your knees to the altars of the saints, but to get down on your knees so that you can talk to a child eye to eye.

One day, a church member, arriving early for a service one Sunday morning, found me, armed with pink rubber gloves and a scrubbing brush, clearing up some vomit left in the porch. 'You shouldn't be doing that,' he said, 'You're the minister!' And of course, I had been thinking just the same thought. But how could we have gone so wrong? Why shouldn't I as much as anyone in the church do such things? It's probably good for me to do it, in case I forget that I belong to a community of equals and that I am called to proclaim the gospel of Jesus, the one who washed the disciples' feet.

I invite you to imagine yourself among the disciples. Imagine the one you call 'Lord' washing your feet. And hear him asking you to wash the feet of others, to give yourself to the way of love he lived so well. And then find the courage to rise on your newly washed feet, and to follow him to Gethsemane and Calvary, to see what it means to give yourself in love for the world. Amen.

Easter
John 20.1–18

When I was first studying theology, some of my teachers put great emphasis on the distinction between nature and revelation. We were told of mysterious pagans who only learned what they could of God through what they saw of nature and what they felt within their bones and within their hearts about the divine. These people, it was somehow conveyed to me, were much to be pitied. They did not know what we now know through what God had revealed in the Bible. I remember looking briefly out of the lecture room window towards the greening trees and the flourishing blossom, listening to the energy of the wind and the sweet song of the birds, and then returning, like a good student, to my books, to the works of the early fathers of the Church and to the serious work of real theology.

But of course at Easter time, nature and revelation are at one. The coming of new life in the spring echoes so perfectly the gospel of the resurrection and new life. The dead, barren landscape of winter comes to life once more. The sharp brown twigs grow rounded green buds and from the brown earth shoot flowers of bright yellow, like little suns coming into every corner of the night and the day. And every year, with the rhythm of the seasons, the spring comes again. And every year, we tell together the story of Jesus Christ, who died and rose again. We strip the churches bare for Good Friday, making them bleak as tombs, and then wake to find them filled with life and colour and flowers at Easter. Love is come again, like wheat that springs up green.

We celebrate today, through water, through the bread and wine, through the reading of the Gospel, and by looking into each other's faces, the mystery of our faith and the miracle of new life. We have to struggle hard to find words which come even close to the joy and the hope which we find here as people of Jesus. We find it hard to describe what it means to find God, to find life, to be filled with Spirit, amidst the sometimes barren landscape of our human lives. So, we speak as though we have been set free from condemnation, declared innocent in court, the penalty paid for us by Christ himself. Sometimes we speak it by telling the story of the people of Israel escaping slavery in Egypt and finding, after many wanderings, the Promised Land. It is like that, we say, to be twice born, to be saved by God. But there is another way of saying it too. It is to echo the ancient words of prophets and of poets who say of the saved, that they shall flourish like a garden. In the book of Hosea, God promises that the people will flourish and blossom like vines. The prophet Zechariah looks forward to the springtime of God's people and says,

> For what goodness and beauty are his!
> Grain shall make the young men flourish
> and new wine the young women.
> (Zechariah 9.17)

In the New Testament Jesus says, 'I come that they may have life, and have it abundantly' (John 10.10). And he promises that, abiding in him, we will become like branches of a flourishing vine. To flourish is simply to flower, to blossom, to be fruitful, to grow, to live. So what we see mirrored in the spring, and what we see displayed so wonderfully in our churches at Easter is the flourishing which is the promise of life. The tree of death, the terrible cross, becomes the tree of new life, and all of us may flower into life as we stand before it and learn its truth.

A flamboyant and lively friend of mine, a man bursting with life out of every pore, spent part of his life in Kuwait. He tells me, with flailing arms and bright eyes, about the spring he knew there. He would gather together friends and they would pack an exotic and delicious picnic and go at early dawn to sit and wait on the bare sand. Then the sun would rise, and on a day splendid with hope, they would watch the desert iris rise from the earth, pushing its shaft of vivid colour through the harsh sand. How could something so delicate, so bright and so full of tender life defeat the deadening weight of the desert? With friends he would toast the beauty of such a moment and tears would overwhelm anyone at such a sign of promise and hope. The desert shall rejoice. Even the landscape of death will blossom into life.

I wonder what it would mean to make flourishing and blossoming our root understanding of what it means to live a life transformed by God? Imagine if we asked not, 'Are you saved?', but 'Are you flourishing?' The abundant life that Christ came to bring, is it yours? We sometimes say, rather cruelly, 'she's a withered old stick' – or 'he's so twisted and dried up'. What would it mean to coax all God's children into the fullness of life?

A while ago, someone sent me a book called *Grain in Winter*, a book written by Donald Eadie, a faithful Christian now severely disabled, who has lived, as he puts it, through a long Easter Saturday, waiting for the spring to come. He describes how, during a long period of convalescence, a discerning friend gave him as a gift an empty white bucket and the bucket became a symbol of his need to be real about his pain, to spit and to curse. Now, he says, after the winter, the spring has come, he has filled his bucket with earth and planted it with flowers! In the book he has collected together lots of sayings, phrases, stories and prayers that were for him like grain in winter, nourishment while the ground is hard and while we wait for spring. My friend wrote in the front page, 'We all need grain in winter.' And so it is. And so it is also true that the spring comes, that it is not, as in Narnia, forever winter. Life defeats the bitterest cold. God comes into the most stinking tombs and brings forth life. And the most powerful and beautiful guarantee of this is the resurrection of Jesus Christ, the first fruits, as the Bible puts it, of the great green harvest to come of abundant life for all.

I am waiting and longing for the Church to be a community where all may flourish and grow, in body and in spirit. I am waiting and longing for a Church that will speak with a bold voice so that the flourishing of some will never be at the expense of others. I am waiting and longing for a world in which all creatures and all things may flourish together, a new green Eden, blessed by God.

God has endless creative power to generate new things, to draw life out of death. Christ is risen. The green blade rises. There is the hope and promise that all will flourish, that the winter of hate and death and discontent will come to its end, and that the spring of God's kingdom will come, in Jerusalem, in our own town, in earth as in heaven. Thanks and praise be to our God, on this most amazing day. Amen.

Ascension
Acts 1.1–11

A few weeks ago I was in a charity shop when I spotted one of my favourite icons for sale. So I bought it, only to discover that a United Reformed Church elder was serving at the cash desk. We laughed at the ironies of ecumenism! The icon is one of the risen Christ, standing on the gates of hell, and hauling Adam and Eve out of their graves. I'm no expert on icons, but this one always catches my eye and makes me think. Adam and Eve of course stand for all of us. They are everyman and everywoman, and the icon teaches the Christian truth that Jesus is not the only one to rise from the dead and to be lifted up on high. That is our destiny too. Jesus' resurrection and ascension are not his alone, but he 'goes first' if you like, so that we can follow. I think it's probably about as central as you can get to the meaning of our faith. We don't have a hero in Jesus, but a saviour. And he didn't come to lift up himself, but to lift us up.

This week a woman told me that she once knew a man she found very irritating. She said, 'He was the worst kind of Christian. He just kept going on and on about Jesus.' She explained that she felt embarrassed and puzzled by these constant references to Jesus and that this man she knew seemed to live in another world altogether. Though I don't know the man of course and I don't want to judge him, I think I know something of what she meant. There are some ways of talking about religion that are very off-putting, and talking about Jesus all the time could indeed be one of them. One of the reasons why it might not be quite right is that you could say that Jesus himself should not be the centre and focus of our whole lives; that, despite what some might think, that's actually not the point of being a Christian.

Jesus spent his ministry trying to open people's eyes to the truth about God and the new world God is bringing. He seems to have resisted those who wanted to make him the focus of everything. He might be the means by which people came to God, but he wasn't the centre of things himself. Perhaps in this is something of the meaning of the Ascension. It was for the best that Jesus finally left, disappeared, vanished from their sight, because in his presence the disciples were too dazzled. They needed him not to be there, at least in some ways, so that they could find their own way, through him, to faith and new life. God's purpose was not that they should stand looking up into heaven at Jesus, but that they should find ways of being lifted up themselves. Or perhaps of allowing the God they had seen in Jesus to lift them up, out of death, misery and the half-light of ignorance, into God's glorious new life. In the icon Jesus lifts up Adam and Eve, with him, out of the grave. They are not to stay in the grave and worship him from there. They ascend and rise to life themselves. So perhaps the Ascension, the departing of Jesus, is a way of saying that we do not need him to be present in quite the same way now and in fact it might even be bad for us. Having known Jesus, heard his teaching, witnessed his dying and rising, we now have to get on with being redeemed ourselves.

There is a very human tendency in all of us to focus on individuals and to long for heroes to admire. Even politics these days has become even more than ever about individuals. As our Prime Minister becomes more presidential so everyone else has to as well. The policies and the manifestoes become less regarded, less read, than once they were. And so much of the talk is about whether or not a particular person could be imagined as Prime Minister. In many ways this is perfectly human and understandable. In other ways it's rather dangerous. But it doesn't only happen in politics. In the stories we tell, in the films we watch, in the fairy tales we tell our children, we have also developed a culture which is obsessed with the individual hero (and much more rarely, it has to be said, a heroine). Again and again in the myths that sustain our culture we celebrate the maverick individual who rises above the crowd. There is a kind of continuity here between the charismatic individuals of the Church's story

like Martin Luther and John Wesley and the individuals we celebrate in popular culture. From Superman to Clint Eastwood's
'man with no name' and Johnny Depp's Edward Scissorhands,
we love powerful and intriguing characters who change the world
somehow. And does it bother you that these kinds of figures are
almost invariably male? It's striking that in many film commentaries now these are described as 'Christ figures', even though the
films are not overtly theological at all. But there is a danger in
seeing Christ in this way, as a 'figure', as an individual, a lone
outsider who changes everything on his own and against the
crowd. This kind of heroic individualism may be seriously mis-
leading for us as we seek to frame and lead our own lives, and
the lives of our communities. It may seem an obvious and very
relevant and culturally exciting way of seeing Jesus, but I fear
that it may be deeply wrong.

The theologian and critic David Jasper has looked thought-
fully at the many films that have been made about Jesus; from
Hollywood blockbuster epics, sandals, beards and swirling music
to *Monty Python's Life of Brian* and *Jesus of Montreal* (see Jasper,
1997). He suggests that the most 'successful' screen stories about
Jesus are those in which Jesus does not actually appear at all, like
Jesus of Montreal, where a group of actors act out the passion
story and find themselves caught up in its meaning, or *Life of
Brian*, where someone else is mistaken for the Messiah. Somehow, ironically, on screen, Jesus is most powerfully made present
when he is absent, and the impact of his life and story is greater
upon the viewer when he is not on the cast list. If present on
screen he becomes a superhero, a Christ figure. But the Jesus who
longed to herald the kingdom of God is most faithfully brought
to us when he is not on screen at all. I wonder if here there might
be a real clue to the meaning of the Ascension. We need Jesus to
be off-stage, so that we can come onto it ourselves. We are not
after all the extras in his story, but we are invited to be players
ourselves. The Christian story is not a one-man show, but a great
mystery play with a cast of thousands who all have a role with
real meaning and significance.

The philosopher Derrida has said something important about
what it means to be a disciple. He was actually writing about

being the disciple of another philosopher, but I think it could just as readily apply to being a disciple of Jesus. He writes about how disciples 'interiorize' their masters, or in other words, take into themselves their masters' ways of thinking and being. Then he reflects on the necessary absence of the master. And he says, 'The disciple must break the glass, or better the mirror, the reflection, his infinite speculation on the master. And start to speak' (Derrida, 1978, p. 32).

In Luke's account of the Ascension in Acts you can sense that Jesus and his disciples are at cross-purposes. They want to know when he's going to do the next heroic thing. He is trying to tell them that they must wait for the gift of the Holy Spirit, and that this gift will fall on them. They are not to keep staring up into heaven looking for him. It is they who now must start to speak, as the Holy Spirit gives them power. You will bear witness for me, he says, to the farthest corners of the earth. The disciples are now to become the main characters. Jesus is not a superhero, a lone figure who will draw our gaze for always. He has gone, ascended, and the stage is now clear for those who follow him. The play is not now all about Jesus, and only him, but it is about the redeeming, the raising up, of all God's people. Jesus is risen and ascended, and this is but the beginning of the rising to new life of all humanity, all creation even. Jesus came not to be a new God for a lowly humanity to adore, but to be the first fruits of a new humanity, a new human race. This truth the Orthodox show in their icon.

In the communion service Christ tells the disciples that his body is now to be shared with them. He will not be present in the same way. He will be absent. But his disciples will become his presence in the world as we interiorize all that Jesus represents and all that he embodied. Theresa of Avila, the Spanish mystic, once wrote, 'Christ has no body but yours.' Only in his physical absence, could this kind of presence become possible. So, I think I see now why there is something odd about a Christian who keeps on talking about Jesus, as though Jesus were the only way in which God could ever be present in the world. The presence of God, known once in him, is now possible in another way. And it is this kind of presence to which the story of the Ascension points. We are not to stand looking up to heaven, but to get on with being present in the world as those who follow Christ, that he may be present in us. This of course is both a great gift and a huge responsibility.

The whole purpose and meaning of Jesus is not that we should have a hero to worship or admire, but that we should be transformed, lifted up, to be what God intends us to be. As Christ reaches out to lift us out of everything that would harm us, let us respond willingly that we, and all God's people, may leave the depths of pain and death and rise to glory. Amen.

Pentecost
Numbers 11.24–30; Acts 2.1–21

The story of Moses and the elders must be one of the funniest in the whole Bible. I don't suppose the makers of the *Carry On* films have paid much attention to the book of Numbers, but if they ever did there is certainly a film to be made. Moses has told God off for being too ambitious. Moses has a hundred thousand men to feed and God has promised yet another feeding miracle. But Moses is suspicious that God will prove to be as unreliable as any other catering company and that he's bound to be let down at the last minute. So God says he'll show Moses just how powerful God is. Moses gets the elders together (all seventy of them) and sits down and waits for the sound and light show. Then God takes some of the spirit he had given Moses and gives it to each of the elders and they go off into ecstasies. It's hard to imagine what seventy ecstatic elders round a tent would be like. I suspect that no one would be listening to the preacher, there'd be no need to bother with the heating, and I suppose no one would think about taking up the collection. But then equally nobody would have half a mind on the dinner or be wondering whether they'd remembered to set the burglar alarm. And all worries about anything at all, any deep pain or sorrow, any fear or anxiety, any depression or loneliness would be caught up, healed, and transformed, in an amazing sense of the presence of God. But there's more to the story yet. Two of the elders, Eldad and Medad, had been left behind and hadn't cottoned on that there was a service going on. But these two were still filled with the spirit, and they did whatever ecstatic prophets do right there in the camp. Someone ran to tell Moses about this strange behaviour and Joshua, Moses' young acolyte, told Moses that he must stop them. You can't, after all, have just anybody being touched by the Spirit of God, especially elders who haven't even bothered to turn up at the worship service! And then Moses says words as profound as any he ever said, 'Are you jealous for my sake? Would that all the Lord's people were prophets, and that the Lord would put his spirit on them!' (Numbers 11.29). Perhaps Moses is a little weary of being the one who has to deal with God all the time. Perhaps he is wishing that the load could be more fairly shared. But more profound than that is the longing for a time when God will not have any kind of special servants, when there will be no especially spiritual people, because everyone will be given the spirit of God. Young Joshua thought it wasn't right that the spirit should be given to just anyone. They might not respect the gift, they might abuse it, they might not be worthy of it. He wants to guard the holy things for particularly holy people. But Moses knows, somewhere deep within him, that that's not how God works. God would have everyone prophets and would give everyone the spirit. It's fascinating that that narrator of the story just feels it must be added that this was the first and the only time that the elders received the spirit. You can take things too far . . . But deeply imbedded in the traditions of the Hebrew scriptures is the hope that one day God will pour out the spirit on everyone, that's all people, no one left out, not just priests, ministers, elders, or even only those who have become members of the community, but all flesh.

When we come to the story of Pentecost recorded in the book of Acts we hear of a time when God's people believed that this day had come. There came a day, on one of the Jewish festivals, when the disciples were all filled with the Holy Spirit. The passing crowds were as suspicious as Joshua. These people didn't look like holy people. They were more like drunkards and most of them with Galilean accents. But Peter managed to find enough calm to tell the crowds that this was what the prophet had foretold. 'In the last days it will be, God declares, that I will pour out my Spirit upon all flesh, and your sons and your daughters shall prophesy, and your young men shall see visions, and your old men shall dream dreams. Even upon my slaves, both men and women, in those days I will pour out my Spirit; and they shall prophesy' (Acts 2.17–18).

Peter knew that in the world as God wants it to be there will be no spiritual elite. You don't have to be a man to receive the spirit of God. You don't have to be of a certain age to receive the spirit of God. You don't have to be wealthy or powerful. You don't have to be of any particular ethnic background. You don't have to be ordained. You don't have to have a theology degree or any kind of degree. Women will receive the spirit of God. Young people and very old people. Even the servants and the slaves will receive the spirit of God. Children will receive the spirit. People you think of as foreigners will receive the spirit.

It is good that at least once a year the Church returns to this story and tells it again. But maybe we need to do it more often. For us, who are in the Reformed tradition, this story is a strong part of our inheritance. For we say in everything we declare about ourselves that the spirit of God is given to all God's people. That's why the church meeting is at the heart of our life together. Not because we believe in democracy (though I pray God we do!), but because we believe that the spirit of God comes upon each of us and that God may speak through any of us. The spirit of God is upon those who come to church on Sunday. The spirit of God is upon those who come to church for prayers in the middle of the week. The spirit of God is upon those who are too ill or frail to come to church any more. Moses said, 'Would that all God's people were prophets and that the Lord would put his spirit on them.' If Peter was right, then Moses has had his wish.

So let us never be jealous or possessive of the Holy Spirit. Let us not guard it only for those with a particular ministry within the Church. Let us not guard it for those with lots of knowledge of the Bible, or for those with perfectly ordered lives, or for those with the loudest voices, or those who say what we have always said in this place. But let us celebrate the spirit's presence with each one of us. Let us share what the spirit brings to each of us so that the whole community may grow in the knowledge and love of God. And let us live as those who belong to a new and different kind of world in which the markers of status and privilege mean nothing among us, because God has poured out the Holy Spirit on all flesh, and all have been blessed with the gifts of the Spirit.

When the Holy Spirit comes it cannot be contained, and if we pray for it then we may be surprised where it comes. In that wonderful story from the book of Numbers, the spirit came upon someone who wasn't even in the building! So today we will pray for particular people who have a new membership or ministry, but we also pray to be given the vision of Moses, who said, 'Would that the Lord would put his spirit on them.' Amen.

All Saints
Ephesians 1.15–23

I would like to address some serious misunderstandings, about the saints. I think that if you were to ask the average man in the street or woman in the pew what qualifications you need to be a saint, then they would almost always get it wrong. So, what qualifications do you need to be a saint?

I suggest that most people would say that you need to be 'dead'. That's a kind of first base qualification. And in some parts of the Church to have Saint in front of your name instead of Mr or Mrs you do indeed need to be dead. And you probably need to have been dead for some time. The last Pope, it is true, speeded things up a good deal. But if you asked most people to name ten saints they'd almost certainly name those who have been dead for centuries.

Most people would probably say that to be a saint you need to be 'good', in the moral sense. That's how the word is popularly used, and sometimes in that sense it's even used of the living. 'She's such a saint to put up with me,' someone might say. And mostly too when people are thinking about the official saints, the ones you could name a church after, they are thought to be good people, or certainly well-behaved people.

As far as the statistics go you're much more likely to be a saint if you're a man, about seven times more likely apparently. Though of course that runs rather counter to experience in other ways (!). But it's certainly the case if you look at any official list of the saints that there are more men than women. So, if you're looking for saintly qualifications maleness is one of them.

You also probably stand more chance of achieving sainthood if you're celibate. Sex might be something the Greek gods excelled in, but Christian saints have tended to live quieter lives. If you're a woman you're much more likely to be a saint if you're a virgin. If you're a man it helps if you give it all up, preferably in a flamboyant and public gesture, for the celibate life.

Saints are also often those who have suffered a good deal, martyrdom being one of the possible entry qualifications. I can't think of many *bon viveurs* among the famous saints, which is ironic really given Jesus' reputation as someone who enjoyed a good feast. Saintliness is usually next to suffering if not to cleanliness.

Saints are also usually thought to be great and extraordinary individuals, quite different from the rest of us. When we think of a saint we tend to think of someone who really stood out from the crowd. A saint is someone who was a one-off. Someone who did what most people could hardly imagine accomplishing. Saints are like hero explorers or great adventurers, the sort of people most of us admire from a great distance. And not the sort of people you could imagine sitting down with for a chat or a cup of tea. Saints are those who are above the crowd.

Saints are also popularly thought to be the famous among Christians. You have to be known to be a saint. Saints are a kind of Christian cult of celebrity. And there are lesser and greater ones just as there are A and B list celebrities. In the Middle Ages, people tended to love best their local celebrity saints, and would leave the big ones to the great cathedrals and monasteries. It's all too human.

Saints are also usually thought of as a kind of holy elite. They are the ones who with the martyrs and apostles will have the best seats in heaven. They are the few shining examples of how human life can be when it's lived as it's meant to be, and not by the usual run-of-the-mill folk like the rest of us.

Of course, I'm exaggerating for effect, but I think I'm not far wrong that in the popular understanding saints are dead, good, celibate, extraordinary, elite, suffering, famous, striking individuals and are most likely male. But what's so interesting is that there is nothing at all like this in the New Testament. Nothing at all. It's true that the Apostles are given special honour and those who were the witnesses of the events of Jesus' life, death and resurrection. True there are some who seem specially favoured, like Mary and the disciple whom we are told that Jesus loved. But whenever the New Testament writers speak of 'the saints', 'the holy ones', there is no suggestion of any of the classic marks of sainthood. The New Testament never mentions once 'a saint' in the singular. All the references, as in the reading from the letter to the Ephesians, are to 'the saints', to the whole community of the Church. The saints are those who are part of the community of the people. They are the living Church, not exclusively those who have died. Since they are the whole collection of people who come to worship and follow Christ, they are not all morally excellent. The sinners are right there among the saints. They are holy ones not because they are particularly good, but because they have been blessed by God, sharing 'the riches of his glorious inheritance among the saints' (Ephesians 1.18b). They are not necessarily celibate either, since any community of Christians is as mixed in that respect as any other. There were women among them in great number and the letter to the Ephesians addresses the 'wives' among the saints as much as the husbands. They were not being martyred. They were not a few extraordinary individuals. They were not an elite among the Christians, since they were simply all the Christians. These are the saints.

If we think of the 'the saints' as meaning only the very special and remarkable ones among the Christian people, only those who have died long ago, only those who have lived lives as we will never live it, this will do our souls very little good. It's good to have heroes to admire, but too often the effect of these star Christians has been to make to make the rest of us feel inadequate and second best, as though we follow Christ in a feeble, pale way. And too often it means that we feel a strong sense of disconnection from other Christians from the past because the only ones we really know about are the hyper-Christians of former times, whom we can only think of as exceptional, crazy or perhaps both. It only serves to disconnect us from other Christians.

But the feast of All Saints is really about recapturing this sense of connection, of discovering our common life with those who have gone before us in the faith. And the feast of All Saints is a wonderful kind of catch-all festival, because it was invented to celebrate precisely those saints who never made it onto the A list or even the B list, but who share with us in the great company of all the saints. For, if the writer to the Ephesians has it right, we are all saints. We are all called to be holy, and part of God's holy people.

We belong to a great tradition which has preceded us and which will succeed us. We are a small presence in a great tide that is more than us and which gives us meaning and purpose. We are among the saints, through past, present and future, on earth and in heaven, in this place and across the great world. We are part of something much greater than ourselves, and in this great community we find a place, a calling, a faith. I find it deeply consoling that I do not have to do everything with my own small life, that the purposes of God are to be fulfilled by the great company of the saints and not by me alone or by my tradition alone! I find it moving to go to Dorchester Abbey and to look at the great list of those who have ministered there, back to the seventh century, and to know that people were keeping faith with Christ in this part of the world that far back. And I find it moving to think that thousands of miles away Christians are celebrating the faith we share in other tongues and in other ways, but with faith and hope. And I find it moving to hope that our children and grandchildren will take up the faith in their turn and in their day.

I am sure that the earliest Christians, when they wrote about the saints, wanted to encourage those who would hear their letters. They wanted to convey to them a great truth, that God was making them into a holy people, dignifying the diverse collection of people who found their way into the early Church, and making of them a holy community. They would have been dismayed to think that this talk of saints might have become anything about special Christians who might leave the rest of us feeling second-rate. The feast of All Saints might be one way of helping us all to know that we are part of something, part of something which will make the best of us, and in which we can find ourselves becoming more fully human and closer to the Creator who made us.

In the New Testament, the word for saints is simply 'the holy ones', that's it. Of course we have tended to make holy mean good, and so holiness has come to mean something like moral rectitude. But holiness isn't the same as goodness. A small boy once described saints as those through whom the light shines. And I think that's pretty good. We're part of God's people, and if we're being God's people, then whatever darkness people are in, it might be that we can be those who let some light in, just as sometimes we need the light too.

So, today let us celebrate, not the famous saints, the extraordinary saints, the titled, haloed, stained-glass saints, but simply all the saints, among whom we have been called to be and through whom God works to bring blessing to the world. We may not be dead, perfectly good, being eaten by lions, or be particularly extraordinary, but we are called to be the holy ones of God. That is both a huge honour and a great challenge, a great dignity and a humbling privilege. May God bless us, who are poor in spirit, as Jesus promised God would, and give us all we need to be a holy people for the world. Amen.

Part 3

PREACHING THE FAITH

A woman as creative theologian

Marcella Althaus-Reid has argued that women have been the traditional consumers of theology and not its producers. So now the time is ripe for women to take up production! One significant place from which to do this is the pulpit. Preachers are what you might call primary theologians, speaking from, for and with communities of Christian people in the base unit of the Church, the local congregation. It is time for women, in their numbers and with their own distinctive voices, to speak out as theologians, and not by whispering demurely or by mimicking the words, tones and styles of their 'fathers', but with the voices they choose and claim powerfully as their own. There have, for some time, been excellent women who work as professional theologians in universities and seminaries (though not yet nearly enough!), but there seems to have been a reluctance among some women to do the work of theology within local churches, to find their own ways of doing the production side of theology in that place so that the faith may be shaped and remade by women as well as men. Sometimes this is expressed as a reluctance to preach or a diffidence about preaching and, of course, preaching is not the only way to be a theologian for a local congregation! But it is still, in the lives of many congregations, an important part of worship, and so an opportunity not to be missed, to speak and shape the faith in new ways.

At one woman's ordination the reading from the Bible was the story of Judith cutting off the head of Holophernes, a brave choice. At one level it was a decision to have a story read about a strong woman, strong in body and resolve. But part of the significance of Judith within the biblical story is that she is a theologian. The traditions of painting, exemplified by Caravaggio and Gentileschi, might portray her as a *femme fatale*, as a courtesan and seductress, but she is more than those things. Her plot to kill Holophernes begins with her reluctance to settle for the fatalistic theology of the male elders of her own people. She refuses to believe that nothing could or should be done to save the people from their own predicament, that their suffering is a punishment sent from God and so simply has to be endured. She refuses to settle for the certainties of those who claim to know what God is thinking. Her intellectual and theological questions have often been overlooked as commentators on this story, commentators of all kinds, have identified her as a seductress and assassin. This may well reflect what, in different ways, has happened to women within the life of the Church, that we are mis-identified, our roles sometimes wrongly (or in a limited way) assigned. We are more readily identified as carers, as pastors, as creative poets perhaps, but not so much as theologians or preachers. While it is true that women will want to do theology in new ways, from different places and in different places, it should not be denied that women have theological voices. We have as much to say about the Trinity as about the care of the dying, as much to say about who Jesus was and is as about justice, peace and the care of creation, as much to say about how to read the Bible as how to pray in warm, lively words. We may want to campaign for doing theology in new ways and in new forms, but it is still theology. So how might women be involved in the making and remaking of the faith?

One way might involve a radical and determined rejection of some of the old separations in the casting of knowledge, a commitment to resist the separations of head and heart, of mind and body, that have characterized much theology in the past. Judith has been identified with the body and poor Holophernes with his head, and so the story serves as a grim parody of the traditional, stereotypical separation of men and women. In resisting this separation women might choose consciously to celebrate the body as a source of knowledge, and the head, as the emblem of reason, still yet as a source of love. The story of Judith challenges a particular theology of the time from which it was written, but it also challenges the presumptions of patriarchal culture and theology that have driven a great wedge between head and body along with 'male/female', 'thought/feeling', and 'reason/experience'. This is what a woman preacher might also choose to do. She can be on the seduction side, but also the production side of theology, and it will be a new kind of theology, saying different things and in new ways. And, just as theology is produced by women, self-consciously and deliberately producing theology from their own lives, so also what it means to be a woman will be changed for the Church.

As I described in the introduction to this book, the Latin American theologian Marcella Althaus-Reid is trenchantly critical of a certain kind of feminist theology, the kind she calls 'vanilla theology' or 'boudoir theology', theology that comes from women with 'lowered eyes'. She calls for theology that will not settle for conformity to the Church's expectations of what is acceptable from women or safe for them. She is like Judith, rolling up her murderous sleeves in the face of theological apathy and faint-heartedness. Her writing encourages women to be much braver than we have been in the past to take up the tools of theo-logical production and to shake off the chains of timid confor-mity. We may be thought 'indecent' (indeed, just like Judith!) but let it be. The terms of what is 'decent' have been set by others anyway and it is time to subvert them. So women who want to preach as decidedly feminist theologians will be prepared, on some days at least, to be radical, to shake the foundations, to speak boldly, not at all 'for the sake of it' but because they will speak from a different place and experience. They will not be timid in questioning some of the mainstream assumptions of theology and culture, because they know that, sometimes at least, these have been based on shaky, patriarchal ground.

In her book *Praying like a Woman*, Nicola Slee writes about

> learning a new language to sing and stutter and shout all we've been aching to say all our lives. And finding how to do it as we do it, learning as we practise, making the way as we walk it. Following no blue print, copying no precursor, we'll craft a jour-ney unpredictable, cast a pattern asymmetrical and intricate, as delicate as it is unrepeatable, tender and indestructible, made of colours vivid, tenacious, wild. (Slee, 2004, pp. 3–4)

Her words could just as surely be applied to preaching as to praying, and they refer, I would argue, not only to the 'style' of what we say, but also to the content and the meaning (though I admit that such a distinction may be hard to hold!). Preaching 'like a woman' will involve a commitment to do it differently and will require courage, for we tread on holy ground. But if we are to join in with the production of theology, then such courage will be asked of us.

David Buttrick, a well-known and much respected writer on homiletics, suggests that in the twentieth century preaching had three directions (Buttrick, in Graves (ed) 2004). There was what you might call 'biblical preaching', which rejected any idea of preaching on a theme or on single verse texts and which saw the main aim of preaching as the interpretation of the Bible for the Church today. He cites Karl Barth and P. T. Forsyth as examples. There was also what he describes as 'therapeutic personalism', exemplified by Harry Emerson Fosdick, a kind of preaching that took its lead from the human predicament, from the needs of the listener in the pew. And finally, he identifies as his third example the kind of preaching that has a social vision, the kind that many black preachers excelled in (Luther King, for example), preaching which stirs the heart to dream of a new heaven and, even more, a new earth. Buttrick has his own vision for where preaching needs to go in the twenty-first century, in which he protests about the increasing individualism he identifies in much contemporary preaching and argues for a restoration of a sense of the gospel promises of God. But this aside, does Buttrick's analysis give us any sense of how women preachers might contribute towards a renewed understanding of preaching as a place where women and men can be theologians for the Church, proclaim good news and contribute towards a renewed, inclusive and peaceable Church?

I have no doubt that many would assume that women's preaching would more likely fall into the therapeutic and personal category, that it will connect more naturally to people's lives and draw on women's often-stated preference for the pastoral encounters of ministry. It could be assumed that they are less likely to be rousing, stirring orators, the kind of preachers to stir emotion or to evoke cries of 'Praise God!' from the congregation. It could be assumed that they will be less likely to focus so much on the Bible, which, after all, has a certain ambiguity for women. However, I would want to resist these kinds of assumptions. I would suggest that women who preach, may, if they choose, do all of these things in determinedly different ways and also, and perhaps more importantly, challenge and undermine some of the distinctions between them. Women may find new things to say about the Bible and new ways of saying those things about the Bible. Women may speak to the personal lives of the congregation, but they will speak to and from the lived experience of women as well as men and with a wisdom that recognizes the locatedness of all human experience. Women may speak of a profound social vision, but they will do that from the perspective of those who have not, in the past, been part of mainstream culture and whose visions have often been marginal or marginalized, whose voices have been repressed, denied and sometimes silenced. They may preach in all these traditions in different ways from their male counterparts. They may also integrate these things much more, refusing the distinction of a personal style or a 'position' in the well-established wars of the discipline of homiletics (to begin with the Bible or experience, for example). They may know, intuit or learn, that text, experience and visionary imagination are always in a circle or spiral with one another and that little is to be gained by seizing on one as the holy grail of the good sermon. Of course, women who preach are no less likely to be varied and different than are men, but we have a particular challenge in beginning to preach, to find our own voices in a discipline which has been regarded, and still is in some places, as the preserve of men.

Barbara Brown Taylor, a teacher of religion and philosophy, and commentator on preaching, writes of all preachers that 'What their congregations need from them is not brilliance, but bravery, as they consent to wrestle in public – and broad daylight – with the same giants that their listeners face alone and at night' (Brown Taylor, in Graves (ed.) 2004, p. 173). She says that a preacher needs to know 'how to be human', that the congregation will want to hear an authentic voice, a voice that 'goes with your body'. If you are a woman who preaches then you are called to preach from a woman's body. You have to wrestle in public and in broad daylight with what it means to be human, and you can only do this honestly if you 'know' that your human experience is not just general and generalizable, but is learned from your woman's body. Thomas H. Troeger writes that 'A disembodied preacher cannot credibly proclaim the incarnate Christ' (Troeger, in Day, Astley and Francis (eds), 2005, p. 121). An embodied preacher cannot, for a moment, forget gender. As women we have learned to know what it means that humanity is gendered, while many men still assume that they can speak, without thinking, for everyone. Women will speak, with awareness, from their own situated experience, and this will mean that their preaching will tell different stories, use different metaphors and reflect different ways of describing the world and searching for truth.

Marcella Althaus-Reid writes of the need for women to use different ways of speaking for God, and for women theologians to be brave in using a language of their own. 'The mutilation of the image of God, using only male language and metaphor to describe God in God's relationship with the creation, is the main reason for women's exclusion from ministry, simply because Christianity has been appropriated as a male religion' (Althaus-Reid, 2004, p. 27). She argues that the ministry of women is still exercised in exile, even if women have been admitted, in some places, into official ministries within the Church. From this place of exile we need not to speak the language of those who have cast us out, but to speak our own language, for the sake of justice and of truth. New theology will require new languages, not bald statements of abstract truths, but the creation of language that reveals that truth is not abstract! If women preach and create new theology in new styles it will not be for 'the sake of it' or to be 'more feminine', but for the sake of the emergence of new truth, new forms of speaking, new theology.

The sermons that follow in this section provide examples of sermons in which a woman preacher has struggled to say something new, to rename the Christian faith or to name it in ways that may convey its themes more faithfully to those who hear as men and as women. They sometimes cross the boundaries of what some would mark as orthodoxy. They sometimes use narrative styles rather than 'straightforward' statement, believing that theology is rarely 'straight'. They sometimes provoke and sometimes seduce. They are all written, and were all preached, with a consciousness of speaking from a different place, from the body of a woman to a still patriarchal Church, in the hope that grace might, as they say, abound.

The first sermon in this section questions a view which is almost always simply assumed, that the judgement made about 'the scribes' as preachers (Mark 1.21–28) was a good one. And in challenging a historical judgement it also challenges the prevailing view in our times that the best speakers are charismatic individuals whose authority is 'evident'. This is a sermon about preaching and authority and offers a new look at what it means to speak of God. It comes from this woman's experience of questioning her own 'guilt' about not being a powerful speaker in the way in which preachers are often urged and encouraged to be. The sermon comes from reflection on experience, on the text, and also on the challenge that some postmodern philosophers have made to the assumptions of our Western culture, obsessed by origins, originality and a certain kind of power.

The sermon which follows, on the story of Naaman (2 Kings 5.1–14), is a sermon that looks at a text by beginning from the experience shared between the character in the story and human beings today, the bodily experience of skin problems. Instead of beginning with history and with leprosy as a 'biblical' illness, it begins with the meaning of skin irritations today, and so interprets the text through that experience. This sermon takes as read that such illnesses have meanings and significance, that illness means more that any physical symptoms, and uses contemporary and very physical experience to explore them. The preaching of this sermon stirred a member of the congregation, a woman who works at an international level for a cosmetics company, to shower me with free samples of the latest creams! This approach enabled the all-too-familiar story to speak to those who suffer today, as their inner lives are written on their bodies.

The story of Simon Peter's mother-in-law (Mark 1.29–31) produces a sermon about women's ministry, which seeks both to dignify the lives of all women and to suggest that the early Church did have a view of Christian ministry that would include women. The sermon works to demystify ministry, and suggest that from the earliest times it was not necessarily a matter of separate orders, but a matter of the offering of service in ordinary (and yet extraordinary) human life. It works to encourage all listeners, women and men, to consider the ways in which their lives are offered as part of the ministry of the Church.

The sermon on Jesus' sayings about children (Mark 9.30–41) uses knowledge of the historical context to ask the kind of 'What would Jesus say now?' question that is dangerous if used too often and too readily, but which can sometimes provoke a revelation. The sermon has a kind of denouement at which the story of an old woman becomes the retelling of Jesus' gospel. It is the experience of many women that maturity lends men respect, but old age marginalizes women yet further. Even in church circles, old women are little regarded, though they are often the core of the church community. How must many such feel when yet more calls are issued for more young people in the Church? This sermon offers hope that Jesus, who placed in the centre the least regarded of his own time, would do the same for those little thought of in ours.

The 'take up your cross' sermon (Mark 8.27–38) is one in which a protest is made about one of the key assumptions of much traditional theology, and this is a sermon spoken from a woman's voice and experience. It echoes the cry of many feminist theologians that it cannot be good news for the humiliated to be told to 'be humble' or for the guilt-ridden to be told to confess their sins, or for the too humble to be castigated for their pride. This is a sermon that reflects on the cumulative effect that a key text like this one has on what the Christian faith has said to many who already suffer, and it asks for a different response. It offers, as one of its moves, a historical challenge to this key text ('Did Jesus really say this?'). But it also offers a theological challenge, asking how it sounds when placed in the wider context of the gospel, a gospel that really is good news for those already labouring under too many crosses. This is a sermon in which a woman's voice speaks to question and overturn one of the cornerstones of traditional Christianity.

The sermon on the story of Noah's ark (Genesis 7.17–23), originally preached in early 2000 at the time of disastrous flooding in Mozambique, begins with the biblical text, but reads it through the witness of a painting by a young woman artist, an artist who 'reads' the story from a particular place. Her own artistic vision enables us to hear the story's dark side in a way that is often covered up or ameliorated by more familiar tellings. She tells it from the point of view of the dead and not the triumphant, and causes the viewers of her work to remain with the drowning rather than to escape, as we usually do, with the rescued. It is shocking that her reading of the story is itself so shocking. What is it that enables us to forget the dead? Why are we so ready to evade tragedy? This reading of the story, provoked by a woman's art, forces us to face these questions.

Exploring some similar themes, the sermon on beauty and violence (Song of Songs 4.9–16 and Galatians 5.22–25) reflects on some of the ways in which we are used to dividing the world into contrasting, and even dependent, alternatives. We do this so readily that the significance of it, as a way of escaping responsibility, is something we can persuade ourselves to ignore. The sermon wrestles with the search for the true world in which beauty and ugliness, love and pain, are held together and not separated from one another, a world in which we all experience both. If religion is a resolute refusal either to condemn or to romanticize the world, but to love and redeem it, then we must find ways to imagine the world differently and to experience it in all its ambiguous reality.

The sermon on the Gospel story of the stilling of the storm (Mark 4.35–41) draws on themes and styles that many might associate with women: the use of narrative and imagination, the lived experience of chaos and dreaming, the search for peace when the storms rage. The sermon takes up themes, stories, experiences and associations that the Gospel text evokes, and draws out the symbolic connections between them. It also draws strength from a hope that perfect calm is not the goal of human

life, but that God can be found beside us in even the most tur-
bulent storms.

The final sermon considers Galatians 3.26–29 and reflects on
the mystery of gender itself. Religious traditions are often assumed
to be conservative when it comes to gender, offering fixed and
unchanging gender roles. This sermon suggests that there might
be room for religion to unsettle gender stereotypes and to offer
a broader landscape in which gender might be playfully remade.
Just as the previous sermon drew upon Shakespeare, this sermon
makes almost as much use of Shakespeare as of the Bible (shades
of *Desert Island Discs*, perhaps!). The main aim of the sermon is
to offer Jesus as an example of someone who, in the name of
God, unsettles gender and liberates us in our struggles with our
own search for gender identity or change. The sermon offers the
hope that the apparently fixed marks of gender may be toppled
by the insistence of the Gospel that these markers look different
in the light of the radical newness and freedom of life in the
kingdom of God.

There are other sermons in the two earlier sections which
also offer examples of preaching boldly 'like a woman', sermons
which change not only style, but theology, by speaking from the
experience of a woman. I hope that some, at least, rise to the
challenge set by feminist theologians like Marcella Althaus-
Reid, that any woman who speaks of faith should not do it with
'lowered eyes' and in conformity with the 'decent' ways of a well-
regulated Church. If the incarnation is true, if the Word became
flesh, then words spoken from my flesh might also, by God's
grace, carry the Word to those who hear. They will be different
words from those I first heard, and different words from those
spoken from other human lives, but I hope that they bear their
own truth. I learn more and more each day, each week, how to
'preach like a woman', as God gives me grace.

Not like the scribes
Mark 1.21–28

They were astounded at his teaching, for he taught them as one having authority, and not as the scribes. (Mark 1.22)

The Chief Rabbi, Jonathan Sacks, speaking on *Thought for the Day* on Radio 4, says that he is sometimes asked, 'Where was God in the Holocaust?' And he would say that though this question is an understandable one, it's really the wrong one. We should ask instead, 'Where was humankind?' God was where God has always been and always will be and God was doing and saying just the same things as ever: 'Thou shalt not kill' and 'Love your neighbour as yourself.' The problem was that people had stopped listening. God continued to give us the freedom and the space to obey the commandments, but we abused it. We stopped listening.

I was thinking about what the Chief Rabbi said when I read this passage about Jesus. The people said that he taught with a note of authority. Which means, among other things, and perhaps most of all, that they listened to him. It means that while on other Sabbaths they sometimes dozed during the sermon or added up the numbers on the hymn board or planned the menu for lunch or supper, that day they really listened. Something in the way he spoke, in the demeanour he had before them, in the way he looked at them as though he knew all about them, in the words he chose or the tone of his voice, something made them listen. Perhaps some of them had not really listened to the Bible or the sermon for years. Perhaps it was all so familiar, a welcome space at the end of the week, a peaceful hour out of the sun. Perhaps it was easy somehow not to listen most Sabbaths, and to hope that the voice of whichever rabbi it was would fill the time and say the familiar things in a pleasant tone. But when Jesus spoke, they listened. And I think that if Jesus really had authority, true authority, then he helped those people to listen to what God was saying. I think that's what true authority means, to have the gift of helping people to listen, not to you, but to the voice of God. And I believe that's what Jesus did. He helped people to listen to God. And it's the things he said and the life he led, the death he died and the new life to which he rose, it's those things that have opened my ears so that I can listen for God. And I hope that you and I will never stop listening, straining our ears to know the truth.

But this Gospel passage provokes some questions. And after remembering the Holocaust they are all the more acute. The verse says that Jesus taught with a note of authority, not like the scribes. There is so much implied in this verse, and we have to listen hard in order to hear it. Unfortunately it's been one of those verses that has, perhaps despite itself, contributed towards the terrible Christian anti-Semitism that has led to many things, including the Holocaust. We assume of course, as we read it, that the congregation are making an accurate judgement, that Jesus was great and the scribes were dreadful, though, if you had been the mother of one of the usual scribes you might have thought differently, I suppose. Perhaps the usual preachers weren't really as bad as all that. But you'd be amazed, or at least I hope you'd be amazed, at what some of the commentators have said about the scribes. They say that the scribes' teaching was empty, flowery and vain, that it was insincere, unfeeling, lacking in passion, less than worthy for the worship of God. But how do they know? It's all too like those commentators who say that the parables of the rabbinic tradition were elaborate and contrived, not simple and direct like those Jesus told. But when you actually read them you find there isn't such a striking contrast at all. The scribes have been given a hard time of it, all in the name of showing, of course, how marvellous Jesus was. And Jesus was, undoubtedly, wonderful, but I think he was so amazing that we don't need to denigrate others to believe that. And the niggle that's at the back of my mind is that I am a scribe. I am a scribe. Let me explain.

Who were the scribes? When we're not busy putting them at the bottom of the class for the Preacher of the Year award, what do we really know about them and the way they did things? It sounds from their name as though they were little more than secretaries, those who could draw up documents. But they were more than that. The scribes were religious teachers, and their name comes from their task, which was to interpret the holy writings, to be readers and preachers of holy Scripture. They were those who had been trained in the Bible and in the traditions of Israel. In Mark's Gospel, some of the scribes are opposed to Jesus, but some are sympathetic. In Mark 12.18–34 there's a story about a scribe who Jesus praises for his judgement about which was the most important commandment. In Matthew's Gospel we meet a scribe who wants to follow Jesus (Matthew 8.19). And there are many things about the way Jesus taught which suggest that he too could have been called a scribe. He quotes the scriptures. He knows them well. He helps people to apply them to new situations and to listen to them as they had never listened before or for a long time. You could say, and maybe you should, that it's not that Jesus was over against the scribes, but that he was a good one.

But there was something else about Jesus. Many scholars would say that he was a charismatic teacher, that he had the kind of authority that people instantly recognized, that everyone there felt that he was speaking directly to them. Usually they expected a preacher to back up his argument with quotes from Scripture, and with traditional examples. But with Jesus that just wasn't necessary, because his preaching had so much personal authority. He was what the New Testament scholar Marcus Borg would call a 'spirit person', and folk either loved him and were completely charmed by him or they were suspicious of him and even angered by him. He was the kind of charismatic man that draws women and men into a close love and admiration or a deep opposition.

Very often the subtext of this story is that the best preachers are really charismatic individuals with passion, personality and so much personal authority that we all just listen open-mouthed, that God speaks best when we are made to listen by the silver-tongued preacher who speaks without a note and who has us all in the palm of his hand (and it's usually a him when we're talking about this kind of rhetoric). Not like those who back up what they say with scholarship, reading and quotations. Not like those who might have trouble being heard in a noisy synagogue or church or who might be nervous in the vestry beforehand. Not like the scribes. Well, I am a scribe, so I have problems with these assumptions. And not just because of who I am.

I think it's one thing to say that Jesus had personal authority, so much that even the demons were impressed, and it's quite another to say that some kinds of people should be allowed to have such personal authority, or that it should be untested and uncritically praised. We have only to look back over the history of twentieth-century Europe to see the dangers of allowing personal charisma to have too much authority. I believe that Jesus had such authority but that the Gospel writers, although they wanted to convince us that Jesus was close to God, didn't want to leave us to find all our hopes in charismatic people. And I also believe that Jesus, like a good scribe, rooted the authority of what he said in the scriptures, in the word of God, in the traditions of the faith he knew. He did not speak a whole new message. In fact there was little he said that was in itself radically new. Rather, by his actions he helped people to listen again to the voice of God, the voice that had been saying the same things for thousands of years, but which we still need to hear again and again, until we have really heard. Jesus had great personal authority, but he used it to say what those good scribes had been saying as well as they could over many Sabbaths, that the great commandment is to love God and to love your neighbour, that we should not kill one another, that we should speak the truth and be faithful to those we love, that God's covenant with his people will never fail. I think the crowd in the synagogue were wrong. He spoke much more like the scribes than they thought. It was just that, for once, they really listened.

Jonathan Sacks has also asked why we are so afraid to mine the great sources of our traditions and our scriptures for the resources we need to live life well before God in this or any land. Why are we, Christians and Jews, so neglectful of the great wells of authoritative tradition that God has given us? We don't have to read them and interpret them uncritically. We don't have to retreat into the past and neglect the new things of our own time. We don't have to be over against modern culture if we are to be religious people. But there are many, many rich blessings to be found in listening to the wisdom of our faith. What we need are not new thoughts necessarily, but people who will help us to listen to what God has always been saying. God has never stopped speaking. It is only we who have stopped listening. We need those who will open our ears to hear again. For us in the Church, Jesus is the scribe above all others who opens for us the scriptures. His authority is rooted in his ability to do this, in his earthly ministry, and in his post-resurrection presence with us. This is the source of our hope.

I am a scribe. I claim no personal authority. I am not a charismatic speaker. I am no tub-thumping preacher. I am no pulpit prince. I appeal only to the wisdom of the scriptures, to the traditions of our faith, and to the continual presence of Christ among us. I do not want anyone to listen to me particularly, but I want them to listen to God. We have seen what happens when people stop listening. And we pray that these things may never happen again. May God continue to be heard among us, through our words and our lives, now and forever, to the glory of God. Amen.

Healing for our wounds
2 Kings 5.1–14; Luke 17.11–19

I have to confess that I have begun these days to take rather more notice of all those TV adverts for skin care. It seems only moments ago that the older women in the Oil of Olay adverts were my mother's age. But now I find that they are my age. The lines are appearing, the crow's feet, the laughter lines, the frown lines. And while some might say that I ought to think about Botox, I prefer to think that I might accept gracefully that my life is written all over my face. My skin tells you something of who I am. And no doubt yours has its story to tell as well.

And very occasionally, when life has got out of hand, like lots of other people, I've noticed that I've had eczema. I once went to the doctor, hoping for a prescription for the latest remedy and she just looked at me pityingly and said something about stress. I realized that the remedy was to be found somewhere else than at the chemist. I have a very good friend whose skin provides a kind of instant readout of what you might call his spirit. I only have to shake his hand and feel the patches of roughness to know that things don't go well. Of course, I know that for many people such conditions have very obvious and physical causes, and that these things show nothing about their spirit at all, but sometimes the pain within us, the inner turmoil, is written all over our body.

Perhaps you saw the TV series *The Singing Detective* or maybe the more recent film with Robert Downey Jr. It's the sort of thing you either love or hate, but take it from the critics at least, that Dennis Potter was something of a genius. In Potter's tale, the main character Philip Marlow has a truly awful skin complaint, the worst kind of psoriasis. He can do little more than lie in his hospital bed, hardly bearing to move his body, which is covered in cracked and weeping skin. But, Marlow is rotting on the inside as well. He is the human being none of us ever want to become. As the story is told we eventually discover that he can only begin to recover when he faces a childhood trauma, the moment when he witnessed his mother's adultery. His disgust at her treachery has been translated onto his skin. He even compares himself to the leper in the Bible and he knows that, in his case at least, the poison of his memories has shown itself on his body. Marlow says that he would have liked to use his pen to praise a loving God, but he can't even hold a pen while he is trapped by the memories that have so distorted his body. At the end of the story, almost miraculously, he comes to terms with the past and he is set free, walking from the hospital a healed man.

The Singing Detective is many things, but it is a story of healing. Just as the doctor gently told me to care for my skin by taking care of my life, so others too have found that what is written on our bodies may sometimes be a story that needs understanding and healing. So, when I read the story of Naaman, commander of the army of the king of Aram, I wonder what story it was that was written on his body. He, like many of us, looked at first in all the wrong places to be healed and to find life again, but eventually, at long last, he found a way. Naaman was a mighty warrior, a five-star general, an alpha male if ever there was one. But, the Bible tells us, he had leprosy. We shouldn't think this means he had leprosy in the full sense. If he had, he would have been out of the barracks and into a leper colony like a shot. What he had was some sort of serious skin condition. Something that was obviously awful to bear, but did not always stop him leading armies and riding horses and chariots. But it was driving him mad, and no doubt his household too. Even his slaves were eager for him to get better, and no doubt he would have been an irritable master with such itchy skin. One of them, a Jewish slave girl captured on one of his campaigns, mentioned to Naaman's wife that she knew a prophet back home who could cure skin diseases as quick as Flash cleans baths. So Naaman set off with a letter of introduction from the King, along with an amount of money that wouldn't shame a lottery rollover, and a wardrobe fit for a film star. You'd have thought he was checking into a five-star hotel or perhaps the Priory clinic. Somehow along the way he forgot the directions and he took his introductory note not to Elisha the prophet, but to the King of Israel, as though he'd turned up at 10 Downing Street instead of Hammersmith Hospital. The King was so insulted that he was about to declare war, until Elisha stepped in, persuaded him there were no weapons of mass destruction, and suggested that he was the one who could get to the root of Naaman's scratching and cure him. Elisha told Naaman what to do, and Naaman eventually listened to the prophet – though he didn't like the sound of it because it didn't seem difficult enough – and he was cured.

Naaman was obviously an establishment man, who assumed that political solutions are always the best ones. But in this case, in his case, he was wrong. We'll never know what it was that was Naaman's problem. Who knows what a wise and far-seeing prophet could see in this soldier's life? But whatever it was, it required from him something quite different from what he expected. And perhaps it was like that for the Samaritan leper too, who would hardly have expected to find healing for his soul and body from a Jewish rabbi.

There are, of course, many problems and pain which find no cure, or which have only straightforward physical causes. But sometimes there are things about our lives that can be changed, and sometimes they are written all over our faces. The sadness may be read in our eyes, the struggle in the lines on our face, the worry in the dryness of our skin. And the cure lies not in creams or surgery, but in finding peace of mind, or a different kind of recovery and a new source of hope. And these cannot be found, necessarily, on the doctor's prescription pad, but in a place where our spirits can be renewed.

And there are those who would say that there are other ways in which the world too can be diseased or wounded, ways be-yond the trials of our individual lives. Naaman and the leper of Samaria were both living in times of violence, of empire-building and war. Naaman was the leader of a great army, a keeper of slaves, a successful, but violent man. The Samaritan leper was a doubly marginalized person, a despised foreigner with an untouchable's disease. His misery was not only his body, but also the situation in which he lived. Some would say that now the world has a kind of 'skin disease', when the colour of a person's skin can still make such a difference to their place in the world, or when a person can be old and wrinkled at 45 in one country, but still youthful in another, or when a bitter and violent terrorist can behead an enemy with a knife. These things too need a kind of healing.

If you think of films you might have seen about Jesus, it's hard to imagine that they would have chosen an actor with bad skin, no blemishes, spots or sores. But in the Jewish tradition there's a very different kind of tradition about the Messiah. In the Talmud there is a story of a rabbi who asks Elijah the prophet where he might find the Messiah. He learns that he will find the Messiah sitting at the gates of the city, among the poor and covered with wounds. The others unbind all their wounds at the same time and then bind them up again. But he unbinds one at a time and then binds them up again, because he knows that he might be needed at any time. The Messiah shares the wounds of the people, but he is ready, wounded as he is himself, to bring healing. And of course in Christian tradition Christ bears wounds on his skin, the wounds of suffering and brokenness, the wounds of crucifixion, bearing wounds so that we might be healed. Today, in Kolmar in Alsace, you can see the great Isenheim altarpiece, a huge medieval painting of the crucifixion which once hung in a hospice for those with a terrible skin disease. The Christ in this painting bears on his body the same lesions as the patients would have done. But he bears them to bring healing.

All of us are wounded, as individuals and as communities. Sometimes the brokenness within us may even be written on our skin, in the wrinkles, lines or wounds of illness. And Christ comes to us not as the one who has skin like a baby, but as one who bears wounds too. And in him we may find a source of healing for our souls, as he touches us with grace. May it be so. Amen.

Servants and ministers
Mark 1.29–31

The story of the healing of Simon Peter's mother-in-law looks to be an easy target for preachers' jokes. Well, it's typical isn't it, a woman known only to us by the name of her son-in-law is healed so that she can get up and serve the tea to Jesus and his friends. Instead of telling her she can put her feet up for a bit, because having a fever and being the subject of a miracle is bound to have taken it out of her, she gets straight on with it and puts the kettle on. It reads like a good go at making 'drudgery divine'.

The woman in this story has no name. She is Simon Peter's mother-in-law. Imagine how different the text would feel if she was named, if it was the story of a Mary or a Lydia or a Joanna. There is a sense in which we do not know who she is because we do not know her name. Then we learn that she has a fever, so bad that she is confined to bed. A fever is generally something fairly trivial to us, unpleasant and inconvenient and justifying an evening in front of the telly or a night tucked up in bed with an aspirin, but the fever this woman suffered might have meant death. She might have been sweating out her life. Mark tells us that they told Jesus immediately about her. 'He came and took her by the hand and lifted her up. Then the fever left her and she began to serve them' (Mark 1.31). The last verb in the Greek ('to serve') is not easy to translate and almost every English translation of the Bible has a different take on it. In this case, my preference is for the Authorized Version, which says, 'she ministered unto them'. The Greek verb used by the writer of the Gospel is a word that is the root of our English word 'deacon', minister. And the Greek word used to describe what she does is the very same one that Mark uses to describe the angels ministering to Jesus in the wilderness, and the same word which the Church used to describe those who served God by leading the Church in prayer and action. So I wonder whether what this woman has done ought to be given greater significance. She ministered to them. Mark tells us that Jesus 'lifted her up'. Perhaps we have cast her down by seeing her only as a 'housewife', or perhaps of course, what we have really done is to downplay the significance of the ministry of hospitality.

And what of ourselves? Many people, many of us, I sense, share with the story of this woman a feeling of uncertainty about the significance of who we are and what we do. And, it may be that through the telling of this story today, and in all that he was and is, Jesus Christ has come to tell us our names and to lift us up, to cure the fevers of self-doubt which may wake us in the night, to give us an identity and a purpose which we did not know we had, to give us a name and a ministry.

There's a Jewish story about Rabbi Yehuda Loew ben Bezalel, who was the greatest rabbi of his age in Europe. One night this rabbi had a dream. He dreamt that he had died and was brought before the throne. And the angel who stands before the throne said to him, 'Who are you?' The rabbi told the angel his name and asked him whether his name was written in the book of the names of those who will share in the Kingdom. The angel read the names, thousands of them, but Rabbi Yehuda's name was not there. He wept bitterly and cried out against the angel. But the angel said, 'I have called your name.' The rabbi protested that he had not heard it. And the angel explained that the book contains the names of all the men and women who have ever lived on the earth, but there are so many who have never heard their true name on the lips of a human being. They have lived believing that they know their names, but they do not hear their names as their own, so they must wait here until they hear their names and know them. Perhaps in their lifetime one man or woman has called them by their right name; they shall stay here until they have remembered. Perhaps no one has ever called them by their right name; they shall stay here until they are silent enough to hear God himself calling them. Rabbi Yehuda woke from his dream and prayed that once at least before his death he should hear someone call him by his own true name.

Perhaps there are many of us who feel that we have not yet met someone who will call us by our own true name, that there is no one who knows us as we are. All of us are defined by what we do, by our relationships with others. We are known as someone's son or daughter, someone's wife or someone's mother, by our job title or even by the role we play in a church. And all of us know how fortunate we are when there is someone who knows us, really knows us, by our own true name. It is one thing to be Simon Peter's mother-in-law. It is another to have someone lift you up and call you by your name and to be allowed the strength to be who you really are, to be the person you were created and called by God to be.

All of us, each one, has some fever, some sickness, something which prevents us from being and offering what we could. Whatever it is, anything from paralysing shyness to the terrible memory of something which damaged you and still does, whatever it is, there is hope for every child of God that some day you will be lifted up, and healed and made well. And all of us have something to give, something precious to offer, to God and to the world. And the life and purpose and gifts of each person should never be despised or dismissed. She ministered to them.

It may be that the Christian Church is one of the last places where being a servant is something to aspire to. Many harassed parents cry out to their children, 'I'm not your servant you know!' and all of us now would hate servility and the ways of living which proclaim some masters while making others servants. But we do believe that service to others, freely offered, and even sacrificially made, is one of the gifts of God's people to the world. And we do believe that every one of us is called by God into being, and so called to be something extraordinary, wonderful and significant, and has a distinctive service to offer to the world.

And of course the chief reason why we value service and servanthood, is that Jesus himself was a servant, one who gave his life for others. As Mark records later in his Gospel, Jesus said, 'For the Son of Man came not to be served but to serve, and to give his life as a ransom for many' (Mark 10.45). And the Greek verb is just the same one as the Gospel uses to describe what the unnamed woman did in her short story. She served as Christ serves. His ministry was echoed in hers. And in the same way it can find an echo in each of our lives, as, in whatever way we are called to do it, we offer service, love, ministry to others.

This story of a woman speaks to us. Jesus Christ comes to serve, and to lift up, to heal and to set free for ministry all the people of God. And the one who is Lord of all, becomes for us the servant Christ, who gives his life that we might live life to the full, and know at last our own true name. Amen.

Whoever receives a child
Mark 9.30–41

> Then he took a little child and put it among them; and tak-
> ing it is in his arms, he said to them, 'Whoever welcomes
> one such child in my name welcomes me, and whoever
> welcomes me welcomes not me but the one who sent me.'
> (Mark 9.36–37)

We're very used to the idea that Jesus loved children and was
kind to them. We've all seen those Victorian pictures of Jesus
surrounded by children. We know him as the 'friend of little children', and what makes a story like *Whistle Down the Wind* so
poignant is that we all know in our hearts that the real Jesus
would really have been excellent with children. We take this for
granted. But in Jesus' own time these sorts of things were not
taken for granted at all.

In the Gospels we find several sayings of Jesus about children.
We know them well and they don't generally strike us as very
extraordinary. Most of you will remember this one from the
Authorized Version, 'Suffer the little children to come to me, do
not hinder them; for to such belongs the kingdom of God' (Mark
10.14). Even with that rather old-fashioned use of the word 'suffer', we know what it means. Jesus liked children and children
are welcome. And then there's the text in which Jesus tells the
disciples that they've got to become 'like children' in order to
enter the kingdom of heaven (Matthew 18.3). And people have
puzzled over exactly what he meant since the day he said it. And
then in John's Gospel, Jesus is even recorded as telling Nicodemus
that he has to be born again (John 3.3), be a child again. And this
too has become part of the bread and butter talk of Christianity.
And, in a sense, it's easy for us to think that Jesus wanted us to

become innocent, new, trusting, joyful, childlike. For us these are very positive things. Not shocking at all. We are shocked not when people are nice to children but when they are cruel to children.

But in the time of Jesus the scene was quite different. We get quite a different feel for what Jesus meant when he asked the disciples to receive children as they would receive him, if we try to imagine what it sounded like at the time. Then we hear the Gospel new. So what would Jesus' sayings about children have meant to the ordinary Galilean peasants or to the Roman citizens who might have heard him or to the citizens of the Greek cities just down the road who had heard a fragment of what he said?

No doubt parents loved their children then as we do now. But if you were born in the first century, it was much less certain than it is now, certainly where we live, that you would grow up. Many babies died in the first hours or weeks or years. This was simply the hard reality of life. And people had to be unsentimental about it. For most people life was a pretty tough battle for survival. We complain now that children are not allowed to be children, but in those days they certainly weren't. In fact the best thing to do was to make it to adulthood as quickly as you could. The best chance of surviving was simply to become useful as soon as you could. Children who were still being children were not very important at all. It was common in the ancient world to dump unwanted babies. Infanticide was something that many cultures practised. Girl babies, but sometimes male ones too, were often left on rubbish heaps, and sometimes they would be rescued, but only to be trained up as slaves. Jewish people were known in the ancient world as unusual because they did not practise infanticide. For many cultures it was simply a practical solution. Children were not treated as human beings in their own right. Indeed, they had no rights, as we think of them now. They had status only through their parents. If you had an import-ant parent you were an important child, otherwise you were a nobody. As far as the ancient world was concerned, childhood was not much more than an unfortunate wait until you reached the age when you could be useful. And this is still something of the reality today in cultures where poverty makes life hard and unsentimental. In our culture too we have learned the hard way, that children are often still treated as nobodies when adults have unchecked power over them. And this is the background to Jesus' sayings about children. He wasn't responding to the cuteness of children. Jesus wasn't tapping into a common perception at the time that children are precious and special. What he was actually doing was taking those who were nobodies in his time and saying, 'If you welcome these, then you are welcoming God.' The things Jesus said about children go with all those things we know so well about prostitutes and sinners, about the destitute and the unclean. Jesus stood with the nobodies of his day and said, 'These are the ones God loves;' 'These are the ones God is blessing;' 'These are the ones you've got to be like.' In Jesus' time a kingdom of children is a kingdom of nobodies. And remember that when Jesus was making this point about receiving children it was just after the disciples had been having a dispute about who was the greatest. He's showing them how they've completely missed the point. They've got to become like nobodies if they're going to inherit the kingdom of God. The whole quest for status and greatness is turned on its head in the kingdom of God.

So where would Jesus go today if he wanted to say the very same thing to the people of our times and our nation? That's never a question you can safely answer. But just imagine for a moment that Jesus is walking around Oxford. He goes with his disciples around the city. He visits the schools, with their new computers and their well-fed, mostly, happy children. He visits the churches with their toddler groups and nurseries. He passes the shops with their designer baby clothes. He visits the colleges as the new academic year begins and the students are arriving, bright-eyed and full of hope. And all the while, behind him, the disciples are having a conversation about which of them is the greatest. Goodness knows what they thought the criteria for greatness were; public speaking, making money, attracting new disciples? Jesus is on his final stop. He shuts the door and asks the disciples what they've been muttering about all the way round the tour. A guilty silence falls. Jesus tells them that if they want to be first, they've got to make themselves last of all. And then he draws one of the people they're visiting into the middle of the room. They're in a home for older people and the woman he puts his arm round is well on in years, she has lost her memory, and she is incontinent. She doesn't know who he is, but she smiles at him and enjoys the cuddle. Jesus seems unbothered by the stains on her dress and the biscuit crumbs on her chin. And Jesus says, 'Whoever welcomes a woman like this in my name, welcomes me, and whoever welcomes me, welcomes not me but the one who sent me.'

I think there could be no more telling way to show today's disciples that the kingdom of God is absolutely for those who are often treated as nobodies in our times. The Kingdom is marked indelibly and always by this valuing of every one of God's creatures no matter how little they are regarded, or how much they are forgotten, by those who hold the power in the world.

Throughout the centuries of Christian history, people have struggled to interpret what Jesus was getting at in his references to children. Some have drawn conclusions that we would find rather bizarre. It's been argued that everyone who follows Jesus ought to be celibate and become asexual, because that's what children are. It's been argued that we ought to be 'mild and obedient', because that's what children at least ought to be. And it's been argued that Christians ought to be naive, innocent, humble. And there may well be something to be said for some of these. But it seems very probable indeed that Jesus was saying something much more basic, and was doing what he always seemed to be doing which was showing that the kingdom of God is a different world from the kingdoms we know on earth. In his own time children were nobodies in a way that, thank God, they are not now. In Jesus' time no one would have thought of including children in religion very much at all. You waited until they were adult enough to take part. In Jesus' time no one would have thought of trying to make childhood last longer or looking to children to teach us wisdom. Children were simply adults in waiting. It would have been felt as an insult for any adult to be compared to a child. Our very different views of childhood are actually staggeringly recent. But Jesus valued those who were low in his time and he lifted them up. He brought them into the centre from the edges. He turned everything upside-down.

In our own time we hear the gospel new. But it is the same gospel. And we find it as hard to hear as the disciples did. We still argue about being the greatest (though usually in much more subtle ways) and we still long for greatness. It's a very human thing. And as we read the Gospel stories of Jesus we discover someone who turned the search for greatness on its head. He valued and cherished the nobodies of his time and asked his disciples to be with them. Who are we to doubt that he would do the same in our time? We may have different nobodies, but we still have them. And those are the people God asks us to serve, to be with, and above all to make welcome. And if we do that we shall be living in faithfulness to Christ.

There are times in all our lives when we experience what it means to be nobody. The gospel is for all of us. Jesus takes us into the centre and shows us that the kingdom of God is for us and that we're welcome, no matter what anyone else says. And we are received and Christ identifies with us. That is the only way in which we become somebodies, through the love of God. The Jesus who received and welcomed the nobodies of his time, receives us in the name of God and invites us to find the nobodies of our own time and to welcome them. This won't make us popular with everyone. It won't make us a mass movement or a raging success story. But it will make us Christlike. Amen.

Take up your cross
Mark 8.27–38

'If any want to become my followers, let them deny themselves and take up their cross and follow me.' (Mark 8.34)

The command to 'take up your cross' has become a kind of motto
of the Christian faith. We take it for granted as a Gospel imper-
ative. We tell each other that we have our crosses to bear and we
encourage each other to embrace suffering. In some contexts it
can be a source of spiritual courage to know that in something
we are bearing we can find echoes of the suffering that Jesus bore
himself. But, for today, I want to suggest that this saying has done
more harm than good, and I want to rail against it, in the name
of the gospel. I realize that I may be treading on holy ground,
but here I will stand.

I know that there are times when it is necessary to face suffering boldly and not to turn away from it. I have profound respect
for those who have the courage to face prison or persecution for
some great good, for those who make sacrifices in a noble cause,
for those who put the needs and hopes of others before their
own comfort or who bear suffering in such a way that it is a
source of encouragement and comfort to others. But I do not
think anyone should go looking for a cross to take up, I don't
think suffering in itself is good, and today I want to accuse the
Church of sometimes engaging in a kind of spiritual masochism
which does great harm. As I prepared to preach this sermon I
wondered who among you I could encourage to take up a cross,
to turn towards some kind of suffering and to take it on. Who
would I choose? I thought of all the people who already have
plenty of suffering and struggle to carry and I resolved not to
ask it of you. And then I thought of all the people whose lives

seem to be on an even sort of keel, and I found I did not want to ask you either. Many of you I know have taken on heavy tasks, which stretch you to the limits. Many of you have been dealt quite enough heavy blows. There is enough suffering in human life already. I find it hard enough to ask some of you to read on Sunday, or to join a committee or to sign up to the coffee rota. How much more then do I find it hard to ask any of you to take on any more suffering than you already carry. And this is not just because I find it hard to ask people to do anything, but because I do not think that it is good for human beings to suffer. I don't think it is good for anyone to take up or to be asked to take up anything that would even come close to the suffering of a cross. And I do not believe that God asks it either. I know that suffering must often be endured. It's part of human life. But I do not believe that the choosing of suffering, in itself, is part of Christian discipleship. I think pain and suffering are, on the whole, destructive things. There may well be saving graces, and any of us can find that we have come through some time of suffering with part of ourselves strengthened. But suffering is not good, it often diminishes and embitters us, and it is not what God made us for.

And yet, in saying this, I am flouting long tradition and I do so with some nervousness. We follow a crucified Christ and we are urged to follow him on the way of the cross. This is usually taken to mean that we too must walk the *via dolorosa*, face and even embrace suffering ourselves. Christianity has traditionally urged its devotees to discipline the flesh with fasting. The Church has been very suspicious of pleasure, taming and even repressing the erotic, forbidding dancing, suspicious even of laughter. Christians of all traditions have been encouraged to suffer, whether it's the wearing of hair shirts, the banning of alcohol, or the bizarre insistence that it is wrong to sit on comfortable chairs in church. These are trivial examples of a serious phenomenon. There are far more terrifying examples of this tendency of Christianity to lurch towards a kind of masochism, which from its leaders also becomes a kind of sadism. The film *The Magdalene Sisters* tells the story of some of the women who were incarcerated in 'homes' for fallen women in Ireland. It's a terrifying story of cruelty and abuse. It was thought somehow that suffering and hard work would redeem these women, but of course it simply provided an opportunity for the powerful and well-intentioned to be cruel and for the vulnerable to have inflicted upon them the most terrible suffering in the name of the crucified one. And let no Protestants think that our traditions have never turned a life-giving faith into something joyless, cruel and mean. They would surely be wrong. In all our Christian traditions, the command that true disciples should 'take up a cross' has brought misery to many, and many who least deserved it.

I believe that Jesus came to set the oppressed free, to raise up the lowly, to open the eyes of those in the dark. He was known as someone who loved to eat and drink, to heal suffering even when he wasn't supposed to and who intervened when the pious wanted to stone adulterers. How tragic and terrible that, in his name, the mighty have caused the weak to suffer and even told them that it would be good for them. Along with many New Testament critics, I wonder whether Jesus ever actually said that we should 'take up a cross'. The saying comes from a time much later when the people of the early Church were desperate to make sense of what happened to Jesus when he went to Jerusalem. I hope and believe that Jesus and his gospel were about delivering the suffering from the crosses they were already bearing and offering them a lighter yoke. He who was heavy laden himself promised rest to others.

The biblical scholar Stephen Moore states it baldly enough, 'The central symbol of Christianity is the figure of a tortured man' (Moore, 1994, p. 95). Where Judaism has a star as its sign and Islam a crescent, Christianity has as its logo an instrument of torture and death. The first Christians, who of course knew much better than we do what the cross 'meant', did not use it as their sign. It took years before Christians could understand the cross as a sign of hope and holiness and salvation. But having the cross, and even the crucifix, as a central image of our faith has had a huge impact upon the way we understand it. Walk round many churches in the world and you will find all too many pictures of suffering, pain and torture, not only of Jesus, but of the saints and martyrs too. We proclaim at Easter that Christ is risen, but for most of the year we keep him suffering on the cross and urge each other to follow him. Christianity is a faith offering new life, the flourishing of human identity, the affirmation of goodness and joy. But too often it has become a call to death, and suffering and joyless dread. The letter to the Ephesians calls us to 'Wake up!' and to 'Rise from the dead!' (Ephesians 4.14). It is this invitation we might choose to answer instead of the command to 'take up a cross'. There are enough pains to bear in human life. Let us not take up any more, unless they will lead to the rising to life of another person or community.

There is of course another way in which Christians have heard the call to 'take up a cross'. But this is a path that is just as disturbing. In the early Middle Ages Christian rulers began to encourage people of all kinds to make a pilgrimage to the Holy Land and to join an army to deliver Jerusalem and to seize it for Christ. They were promised an easier passage to heaven if they took up arms. And somewhere it began to happen that the pilgrims sewed on to their clothes the symbol of the cross to show that they had committed themselves to this path. And as they went into battle, often simply to be slaughtered in their thousands, the banners of war carried the sign of the cross. 'Take up your cross' became a rallying cry to take up arms in the holy crusades. And for us today, standing on the brink of another war which will surely be seen, even if it is not intended to be, as a war of West against East, of cross against crescent, the call to take up the cross must make our blood run cold. Again we might say that there is enough suffering in the world. It would be terrible beyond measure to inflict more of it on anyone, and least of all in the name of Jesus Christ. Sometimes suffering is necessary, sometimes it is inevitable, sometimes, exceptionally, redemptive. But we must never by our loose way with words imply that it is less than terrible or forget that it is, at almost all costs, some-thing to be delivered from and not embraced.

At Communion we remember the story of the one who did walk the way of the cross, whose body was broken and whose blood was shed. In a way that Christians have always found it hard to explain, we believe that his death was somehow saving, that something about his dying might bring us to our knees in gratitude for the love that God has shown to us. But I do not believe that Christ went to the cross so that we should go to a cross as well. I do not believe that he died so that we might die, in pain, lost and suffering unbearably too. I do not believe that if we are true Christians we must look for a way to be crucified. The gospel tells us that Jesus died, so that we might live. Jesus bore pain, so that we might be set free from it. Jesus carried his cross, so that ours might be lifted from our backs. He was heavy laden that we might find rest. If we look to take up a cross we find that Jesus has already carried it for us. If we choose to deny ourselves, we find that God wants to give us back life in all its fullness with splendour and joy. Our God is the God of life, of freedom, of joy and of hope. God comes to bring healing for pain, comfort in sorrow, new life where we have dried up. God promises blessing, fruitfulness, life and an everlasting covenant. We are heirs of the promise and God's promises never fail. Amen.

The deluge
Genesis 7.17–23

I guess that if we were sitting in Mozambique or Madagascar right now, we would find today's Bible texts bitter reading. God promises never again to destroy the earth by flood. God makes an everlasting covenant. But today the rains still fall. Some of the richest agricultural land of Africa lies submerged under flood water. And even as the rescue attempts begin, even as aid arrives, more rains fall, as though to taunt the suffering. We cling to signs of hope. A baby is born in a tree. But her grandmother was swept away by the waters and drowned. Thousands upon thousands are homeless, many have perished. The mosquitoes multiply. Crops are destroyed. And God seems far away. In Madagascar they are frightened of rainbows. There is little for their comfort as the sun's light is reflected through the rain.

The story of Noah is probably the Bible story that adults most readily tell to children, the one children know best and which is modelled for them in toys and nursery books and songs. Every child knows that the animals went in two by two. The lucky ones have a model of the ark with pairs of exotic animals. When I was at school we all sang 'Captain Noah and his Floating Zoo' by Michael Flanders and Joseph Horovitz. The story is the toddler's favourite of the Bible. But the story of Noah is not as cuddly as a Beanie Baby. The story of Noah and the Ark is also the story of genocide. It is also the story of the countless ones whom God destroyed. This is the darkest story of the Bible. You could be forgiven for thinking that it should be kept from children, lest they should fear the terrible God who destroys. In the light of the experience the world is watching now, we should all be afraid that the flood has returned, that God is either against us or absent, that the everlasting covenant and promise of God has been broken.

We are too used to seeing the story of Noah and the Ark in bright, sunny colours, right for the nursery. We have forgotten its darkness and terror. But there are those who can remind us of this story's power. They will enable it to speak to us again, to speak to us in the midst of the tragic scenes we face even today. There's a picture in Tate Britain, painted by a woman called Winifred Knights. She painted it in 1920 when she was 21 years old. It is called *The Deluge*. Knights produces a kind of ruthless picture and excludes so much of what we have come to expect of such a painting. There are no pairs of animals. There is almost no colour beyond a range of greys. There is little texture. Even the brick and glass and water have none. There is almost no detail and the buildings and the ark in the background are almost blank. She offers us no comfort. The ark is sealed up, a sharp-edged colourless shape, floating away into the far corner. She shows us not the saved, not Noah and his family, but only those people who are being overwhelmed by the flood. Some of them reach for their children or struggle to climb impossible slopes to safety. Others reach out their hands, perhaps to God. But we know that there is no hope for them, that they will achieve nothing. They can only mime their helplessness. The world around them is already dead, the colour of it gone, the crops in the field in the middle distance will soon be destroyed by the rain. The picture is actually huge, five feet by six, the height of a human being. Its impact is one of terror and bleak despair. This is a part of the story of Noah which she helps us to find again.

The only thing in the picture which offers us, the viewer, anything at all is a little girl in the middle of the picture, a little girl in a rust-red dress with curly golden hair. Unlike everyone else in the picture, she looks out of the painting and she looks at us. Does she challenge us to understand this story, to turn from our wickedness so that it won't happen again, or perhaps to remember the tragedy of the story, to remember that those who perished and who perish still today are children and parents and grandparents, people like us? Or does she simply plead with us to let her live. I am colour and curve and life and I want to go on. I want to live. She acknowledges that we are here, that these great myths of our tradition belong to us too, that we are part of this story. And maybe she tempts us to have compassion for the drowned ones and to hope that, despite what God has decided, she might manage to survive the flood. She is waiting for the rainbow.

The film *Schindler's List* was based on the book by Thomas Keneally called *Schindler's Ark*. It tells the story of a Gentile businessman, Oscar Schindler, who managed to save hundreds of Jews from the Nazi Holocaust, by employing them in his factory. It's a true story. Schindler was no saint, not a righteous man in the biblical sense. His factory made him money and kept him in with the regime. He was a philanderer and a playboy. But he risked his own neck to provide a safe place, an ark, for many Jews. While many ignored the flood of terror all around them and tried to save only their own necks, he saved others. Stephen Spielberg's film of the book, like Winifred Knights' painting, is almost completely without colour. It is made in black and white. But in the middle of the film there is a scene in which we watch a small girl trying to run away from the terror in the Ghetto as the Nazis are trying to clear it. We must watch her because she is wearing a red coat and this is the only colour in the film. She is a beautiful child, and we hope that she will escape. But later, the small, red coat is seen again, amongst the dead. And, oh how we wish, more than we knew we could wish about a character in a film, that she could have lived. Why couldn't she have survived? Why couldn't she have made it into the ark?

We live in a world in which millions perish, both because of natural disasters like floods and because of human wickedness like the Holocaust. And it is hard to believe that there is a good and holy God at work in such a world. Providence frowns at us. The authors of the book of Genesis do not hide from us the terror of the suffering, or even the terror of God. They leave us to struggle in the darkness, in the place like Winifred Knights' painting, where there is little of the colour of hope. It is tempting to escape, to pretend that it is all right because some people made it and still make it into the ark, or some ark or other. It is easy to celebrate the salvation of Noah and his family, but the story, as the Bible tells it, leaves us to grieve for the lost and to reflect on the kind of God who could wipe out almost everyone. Or even just to reflect on a God who cannot prevent the genocide and the flooding, the sickness and the pain. There is a story that one night in Auschwitz a group of Jews put God on trial and found God guilty of permitting the obscenity of the death camps. They condemned God to death. But, when the trial was over, the presiding rabbi announced that it was time for evening prayer. Even in the midst of terrible suffering, even when all hope would seem to be lost and when every ark has been sealed and has sailed away, there will be faithful people who cannot forget the colour of hope, who go on in the faith that somewhere, behind the frowning providence of tragedy, God hides a smiling face. We who number ourselves among the hopeful, hold on amidst the flood and wait and wait for the rainbow.

But taking the tragedy of the world seriously, hearing the story of the Flood as though for the first time, will mean that there are some ways of religion that we will not choose. In the first letter of Peter (1 Peter 3.21), the author seems to imply that baptism is what brings us to safety, a new kind of ark. But while we know that baptism brings us into the Church, it does not mean that suffering will not touch us or that we are 'saved' while the rest of the world is lost. We will not celebrate our own safety and gloat over the perishing of others. We will remember instead the story of Abraham, who pleaded with God to spare the citizens of Sodom and Gomorrah and not to sweep away the righteous with the wicked. We will live as he lived, making courageous pleas for the suffering, both in our prayers and in our deeds, and not as Noah, who apparently made no such plea and who simply saved his own family. All too often, religion encourages us to concentrate on those who are safely within the fold. But we, who are followers of Christ, will surely follow him into the places where people are suffering and afraid, where people are being lost to themselves or to God, where people are drowning for lack of hope. We will, if courage is given us, not cling to the safety of an ark, but turn boldly to help those who are drowning. There are Flood stories in many religious traditions. In one, even more ancient than the one in our Bible,

Utnapishtim, the sole survivor, tells of his desolation when he finally climbed out of *his* ark. When he saw that all 'of making returned to clay' he wept, with tears running down his face.

The suffering of our world deserves our tears and our honesty. It deserves our prayers and our protest and our deepest questioning. It also demands from us a response. The people of God hold the hope that there is a rainbow that will shine through every pain and that God has not forgotten us. The people of God will not seek only their own safety, but the redemption of all the world. The people of God will risk even themselves to help the drowning. For God has shown us in Jesus Christ that God will not turn from suffering, but will embrace it and transform it, for the sake not just of a few elect, but for the whole world. Amen.

Beauty and violence
Song of Songs 4.9–16;
Galatians 5.22–25

As I think about it, I realize that there are two Lebanons in my head, and that I have trouble holding them together. I've grown up with the Bible, and I'm a big fan of the Song of Songs with its beautiful poetry and images. So I have always known, since I can remember, of the strong and beautiful cedars of Lebanon, trees strong and fine enough to build a Temple. I remember how the bridegroom and bride praise each other for their beauty, beauty like Lebanon, choice as the cedars. I can picture its lush valleys, fruitful trees, scented gardens and graceful people. But also, too often, I've seen news stories from another Lebanon. I've seen pictures of a bullet-pockmarked and bomb-exploded Beirut, a city so devastated and grim that no one could ever think it beautiful. I remember so well the stories of the hostages, and have a strong mental image of Terry Waite chained to a radiator in a dark basement. I have read Brian Keenan's memoir *An Evil Cradling*, and I've seen pictures of banners the colour of blood hanging in the streets claiming 'Divine Victory', banners which move in the wind while the bodies in the streets lie still as death. So I live with two Lebanons, the gentle and beautiful Lebanon of my Bible-fed imagination and the fearful, violent Lebanon of the news channel, where brutality too terrible to tell has scarred the land and its people.

The travel writer William Dalrymple has described his first experience of the Bekaa valley (see Dalrymple, 1998). From above it seemed so beautiful, with water meadows and long lines of poplars, and beech trees all turning with the colours of autumn. But as you go down the valley, the impression of a pastoral oasis disappears. Rubbish lies like a carpet on the ground, carrier bags are caught on the barbed wire, and wrecked buildings dot the roadside, neither repaired nor demolished since some long-ago battle. The country of cedar and scented flowers is also the country of opium, heroin and Semtex. There are beautiful Lebanese faces, but many Lebanese bodies and souls bear the deep scars of terror and war. The constitution appoints always a Christian president, but now Christians are a minority community in the Lebanon, and they live at this moment in terrible dread of yet another war, for they know that their neighbours will surely turn on them, thinking that, if they are Christians, they must be allies of the United States. How can it be that such beauty and such violence exist together? How can it be that I have lived with two Lebanons? How can we hold them together? And does it matter that we should?

It is a very human thing to divide the world and our experience into opposites and into parts. We like to speak of goodness and evil, of enemies and friends, of male and female, of physical and spiritual. We see it most starkly of all in the stories we tell to our children and even to each other. In fairy tales we know who is evil and who is good. We know who to cheer and who to hiss. And it's almost always the case in fairy tales that the good are beautiful and the bad are ugly. We know, and we almost do not need to be told, that Cinderella is beautiful and that the ugly sisters are bad. It's a kind of code that we use. In the film of *The Lord of the Rings* the orks, the enemies of the elves and the hobbits, are profoundly ugly and dreadful, so that we know they are bad. Violence and ugliness and evil go together in books and stories and legends. And goodness and beauty hold hands as well.

But in real life, and in some of the better stories, things are not so simple. The Lebanon of beauty is the same Lebanon in which the terrors and the wars have taken place, and it is the beautiful Lebanon that is also scarred. We might like to divide the world up into different kinds of places, evil empires and the lands of the free. But it is not so simple and never could be. The beautiful people of the Lebanon have suffered ugly things. Some of them have done ugly things. It is hard now for the best informed of us to unravel the politics and the reasons and who is on whose side. But the fighters and the factions are part of the beautiful Lebanon, and the beautiful valleys are also the home to terrible suffering. They are connected and entwined and we must not forget either one in our praying and thinking.

Throughout human experience we have tried to separate things out and to divide one thing from another. We think of God being up in heaven, while we live down on earth. We separate beauty from violence. We put our prayer in a different compartment from what we do. We think of spirituality and action as two different things. This is the way of thinking to which we have become used. But the faith we have inherited, and the faith we share with the Christian women and men of the Lebanon, says something different. It says that these things are not to be held apart, but that all these things belong together. At the heart of the Christian faith is a belief in incarnation, that God became flesh and, against all the instincts of human beings, brought together what is divine and what is human. In Luke 1.26–38 we hear the story of the angel coming to Mary and telling her that the Holy Spirit will come upon her and she will become pregnant. In our world, we have held spirit and body apart as though they are quite different things, but in the world of the Bible, they are held together. The Spirit anoints Mary, but it's not only a spiritual experience, it's a physical one as well. And Paul, writing to the Galatians, speaks of the gifts of the Spirit. For him a spiritual experience is not a warm cosy feeling, but is something that means that you will act in a different way, that you will live a different life in very practical ways. Spirituality and action are not different things, but held together. The spirit is not something out of this world, but rooted within it. The Holy Spirit blows not only in the beauty of the Bekaa valley, but also among the carrier bags on the barbed wire and upon the people shattered by its suffering. God is not only in heaven, but God is also and profoundly at work upon the earth.

So today we are praying that the Holy Spirit will unite us with the Christians of Lebanon, and with all women and men in that place. If war does begin again in that place it will affect all of us, here and all over the world. Our hearts must long and our lips must pray that the beautiful valleys and the strong cedars will not shudder once more as bombs fall or shake as they hear again the cries of grieving women because terror strikes. Let violence be no more in the land of such beauty. Let faith and hope and peace find their voice again. May the Lebanon we have known in our times be known as a Bible land of beauty and strength. Come Holy Spirit, come. Amen.

The tempest
Mark 4.35–41

I jump off the boat into the cool, clear water, as blue as sapphire and as transparent as glass. I make a big splash because it is a long jump from the end of the boat. I let myself drift into the deeps. Startled fish swim away from me and the salt tastes strong on my lips. Rising to the surface, I swim lazily, letting the water cool my body. In the water, and by these caves pregnant with myths, I muse and sigh. I look up at the people on the boat. Others are now coming in. One woman is very fat and her large legs are mottled and veined, but as she jumps she is beautiful and brave. Most of the others watch from the boat and some of them are laughing and pointing. They cling to their clothes and their cameras, to the safety of the modern world and the possibility of the bar, but I am lost to the deeps. I do not know how deep the water is below me and I do not care. For a moment I wish the boat would sail away and leave me here, in the waters, in the deep, where I am weightless and lovely and being is bearably light.

Suddenly, strangely, the wind is stronger and the cool, blue water moves more quickly. The captain summons the swimmers back to the boat. The water is murkier now and already clouds have darkened the sun. For a moment I am afraid and I reach too quickly for the ladder. Slippery with the sea, it escapes my grip. I imagine mythical monsters at my heels and the strong pull of the sea, as cooler air brushes my cheek. But soon I am safe, and the music from the bar is louder than the winds. Later, drier, looking back, I think to see danger in the churning waves, but in the seat opposite me in the noisy, rolling boat, is a man, fast asleep on a cushion.

I have described an experience from a holiday in Greece. A beautiful day and a memorable one, but also one in which I sensed the beauty and terrors of the deeps, and maybe not only in the ocean, but also in myself. And as all experiences always do, it came to me not just as itself, but through the books I have read and the stories I have been told. As a storm threatened off the island coast and as I watched a man sleep undisturbed by the wonder or the threat of it, I remembered the story of Jesus asleep on the cushion in the boat. And I also remembered another story, Shakespeare's last play, *The Tempest*. I remembered how Prospero and his daughter Miranda were banished in a leaky boat and found themselves sharing an island with only a spirit and a base creature for company. And of how the play begins when those who had banished them are in turn caught in the midst of a storm. The noblemen from Milan are frightened on the storm-tossed ship, and cry out to the sailors to save them. But the sailors protest that the sea will have no regard for their nobility. The sailors believe there is no one who can control the terrible and unpredictable forces of nature, forces that have no regard at all for rank or deserving. But then we discover that the tempest has actually been caused by the magic of Prospero, who with all his books represents the highest culture and civilization. At the end of the play he vows to still the waves, but finally Prospero's powers are limited, and he prays to be released from his exile. There is a critical storm about this play. What does it mean? Some will say that it is about European domination of the natives of the New World and Prospero is the terrible oppressor of a more primitive people who are represented by the creature Caliban. Others will say it is about the relationship of nature and culture, of chaos and order. It's a political play about the terrors of colonialism or it's a play with universal themes about the deepest parts of our psyches. And, of course, it could be, and is, both. But we all know, I think, the feeling of being 'all at sea'. We all know times in our own lives when the storms rage around us, and all the 'resources' we have gathered around us of culture, of faith, whatever it is, seem to have nothing to say to the gale of suffering and struggle that we face. And then sometimes we do know what it is to find that those things deep within us of faith and of meaning wrought from experience, that those things *do* hold us in the midst of the storm, even so that we can be still and survive the buffeting of our little and fragile boat. Sometimes we are Shakespeare's sailors, convinced that nothing can save us from the storm, and sometimes we are Prospero, knowing that 'Though the seas threaten, they are merciful' (Act V, Scene 1). The disciples were, like all sailors, afraid of the sea. Not just afraid of the natural patterns of creation, of the winds and storms that sometimes rage even in gentle Galilee. They were afraid too of the forces of evil and chaos, the powers of the deep, the powers that sometimes threaten all of us. They saw the wind and the sea as forces with wills to obey or disobey. They saw them as the repressed chaos before the orderly, rational creation. They were afraid of the squall because, for them, it was the devil mocking their Lord. They saw the sea – the sea, as the place of chaos, of disorder – and they were afraid. They saw in its tempests and moods the thrilling and terrifying dramas of their own lives and fears. In early myths, the orderly God hovered over the face of the waters and made, from the world of chaos and monsters, an ordered creation and such an order they wanted to preserve, an order in which sinners are different from saints and in which God can control and sub-due everything in us and in the world. And so they cried out to Jesus to stop the storm and calm the chaos, to be like Prospero, a sorcerer of the deeps. But Jesus is not worried. He is not dis-turbed by the chaos. He sleeps peacefully. He is all right, even as the boat is tipped and rocked by the forces of the deep. He sleeps and drifts and takes his ease, rocked to sleep by the chaos that wakens only their dread. He sleeps, he sleeps, as the billows roll and all is well. The anchor of his spirit holds, though the boat is storm-tossed. 'We are such stuff, as dreams are made on, and our little life is rounded with a sleep' (Act IV, Scene 2).

A child rushes to her mother's bed in the mornings and tells of all the terrors of her sleep. We, all of us, have dreams and nightmares of our own, storms of the psyche and tempests of the heart. And in all such storms we cry out for God to come and still the waters, to drive out the chaos, to calm the storm. But God comes only sometimes to quell the storms. And more often to teach us to sleep through them, to be at peace with whatever storms assail us, to live with whatever comes, and to be at rest, though the storm rages round us.

There is a fascinating and odd little phrase that is part of Mark's account of the stilling of the storm. It is so odd that some translations leave it out, though it is definitely there in the Greek. As the story is set in Mark, Jesus has been preaching for a long time, from a boat at the shore's edge. He has told them several of his best-known parables. Now evening has come and Jesus says, 'Let us go across to the other side' (Mark 4.35b). And then the Gospel reads, 'And leaving the crowd behind, they took him with them in the boat, just as he was' (Mark 4.36).

The puzzling phrase is that 'just as he was'. Why is it there? Presumably, you could say 'without going ashore', but it's hard to see how that explains it. Or perhaps it's there just to remind readers that Jesus is already sitting in a boat. They might have forgotten because they were told so long ago, and somehow it has to be explained that he doesn't need to get into a boat to cross the lake because he is already in one. But maybe there is a simpler reading. It struck me, noticing this phrase for the first time, that it almost seems to suggest that Jesus went 'just as he was', in the clothes he stood up in, you might say without his sailing clothes, with no kagoul, no warm cloak, no preparations for a sail on the stormy and unpredictable lake. He went 'just as he was'. But still, unprepared and unready as he was, he managed to sleep peacefully while the storm raged. He went 'just as he was', a man, not a sorcerer, not a Prospero, just as he was. But still, and perhaps because he was most fully and most straightforwardly a complete and faithful human being, anchored in God, he could be at peace in the storm. Just as he was. You do not need to have magical powers to find the peace of God, but to come before God just as you are.

Charlotte Elliot's famous hymn 'Just as I am' encourages us to come to God just as we are 'though tossed about with many a conflict, many a doubt'. And if we come as we are, God will hold us in the tempest, and the breadth, length, depth and height of God's love will prove more than equal to any storm. God does not, like Prospero, promise us always calm seas and auspicious gales, but God will be with us in the storms and bring us God's peace. Amen.

Twelfth night – or what you will
Galatians 3.26–29

'I am all the daughters of my father's house, and all the brothers too . . .' (*Twelfth Night*, Act II, Scene 4)

In Shakespeare's comedy written for the revels of twelfth night, Viola is only her 'real' gender in one scene. In all the rest she is disguised as a man and calls herself Cesario. Her disguise leads the plot into many twists and ironic turns, all given a double edge when we know that when the play was first performed all the characters would have been played by men. We have to imagine watching a man play a woman who is disguised as a man who is later revealed to be a woman. Gender confusions and cross-dressing are common features of many Shakespeare plays, but in *Twelfth Night*, they are central and they reveal a truth to us; that gender is in real life, as it is on stage, an unstable mask. There are many places in which the text tries to define the boundaries between the genders. Orsino, in the second half of Act II, Scene 4, tells us that women's passions are not so strong as his own, that women's hearts lack retention. Even Viola (as Cesario) admits that men say more and promise more and she assumes her own subordination to men. But the evidence of the story is that the assumptions we make about gender are often false and that we are easily fooled, that gender is an unstable mask. The text tries to police the boundaries of gender and at the end all the couples are put right so that everyone is paired up with the 'right' gender. But this play also disturbs the boundaries. The cross-dressed Viola, the woman who can sing both high and low, the woman who is easily the most interesting and wonderful character in the play, with the best speeches, and who is loved by a woman and by a man, puts in question the fixed nature of sexual difference. She can indeed be all the daughters of her father's house and all the brothers too.

St Paul famously declared that in Christ 'there is no longer male and female' (Galatians 3.28). But who was he kidding? In the film *The Crying Game*, a man discovers that the beautiful woman he has been falling in love with has a penis and he throws up in the bedroom sink. It matters to all of us what gender we play. The taunts of children, the fortune we spend on making gender look good, the vulnerability we all have to those who might misjudge who we are. Hayley, the transsexual character in *Coronation Street*, has movingly conveyed some of the pathos and agony of feeling yourself the wrong gender, and the publicity around her story demonstrates the anxiety and fascination this subject creates – though why could she not be played by a 'real' transsexual? Enid Blyton's famous five enact for us some of the negotiations of gender as girl readers decide whether they are more like Anne or George. Our gender is something we explore, grow into and sometimes enjoy. Dolly Parton, the country and western singer with the famously surgically enhanced body, says that she loves being a 'girl' and that if she hadn't been born a girl she would have been a drag queen. Being a woman is something she 'plays'. Gender is performance as much in life as on the stage, and there are choices about the scripts we choose to learn or even the scripts we encourage one another to write.

We leave gender largely unthought within the Church, though discussion runs high in our culture. And the Church has its own scripts about gender which it is time to read more critically and more creatively. Because gender (and sexuality) are not fixed, given and innate entities. There are not traits or characteristics that are inevitably and eternally 'feminine' or 'masculine'. I want to resist those who say that the genders are complementary (as Orsino no doubt would have done), a judgement which always seems to leave women in the second place. But neither is it simply 'all in the mind': we do not have anything as simple as a free choice about how we live out our gender, as many a transgendered person will tell you. We are all born into a culture in which gender is constructed in particular ways, and even as we learn to speak we are made. Even our most apparently fundamental experiences, birth, sex, pain and death, work and learning, come to us already mediated through the signs of our culture. But we are not only observers of gender, we are also its creators. We are constrained, but we may also be active, and gender is constantly being fought over and remade. There is room for negotiation, for subversion and critique. The creation of gender is incomplete and it happens on the stage of the world and of the Church. And in the Christian tradition we have stories of our own which can help us recreate gender.

Moses, like Viola, was rescued from the water. His gender was the reason for his abandonment, as all the little Hebrew boys were to be killed. Gender can bring death as Viola knew. And for gender, Moses ranks as the hyper-male, bass-voiced, a mighty-man-of God. In the story of Jesus, performed upon the stage of the Gospels, we are given a more ambiguous sense of what it means to be gendered and human. Jesus is never portrayed in the same macho style as Moses. Many times you can see in the minister's vestry or in the church hall pictures of a remarkably feminized Jesus. The beautiful long hair, the elegant hands, the serene expression. All stereotypically feminine characteristics. And the Victorian paintings have a curious affinity with the asexual clown of *Godspell* or the main character in that film *Jesus of Montreal*.

These images of Jesus embody a gospel truth. However hard we try to repress it, the gospel returns. The miracle of the incarnation is that God became flesh, human flesh. The many and varied portrayals of Jesus reveal the truth that all of our humanity, wherever on the male–female spectrum you find yourself, has been redeemed and experienced by God. The androgyny of Jesus, Jesus the man, Christa the woman, all point to the gospel truth that we are all saved, all touched by the grace of God. In Christ there is neither male nor female, or rather there are both and all shades in between. Jesus is only fairly portrayed as a new Moses if he can be a new Miriam too.

Even the Gospels themselves, even they, from a world quite unused to our own style of gender-bending, present a Jesus who is a new kind of human being. Here is a man who claims for himself words and experiences from female experience. 'How often have I desired to gather your children together as a hen gathers her brood under her wings' (Luke 13.34).

He talks with women. He takes their side. He listens to them. He befriends them and welcomes them as his disciples and inter-preters. As he goes toward the cross, Jesus is silent and passive, taking what would have been seen then and many have seen since as the feminine role. 'Behold the man' says the Gospel, but some-times Jesus plays it like a woman. And when risen from the dead he appears to women and makes them his first witnesses, even though their gentle voices were silenced and they were afraid.

Most of us are pretty afraid of gender and frightened to play it differently, and that's to say nothing yet about sexuality. But some of our most profound experiences of suffering and of joy and self-knowledge come from our awareness and practice of our gender. Jesus was unafraid to play it differently and he/she, risen and ascended, speaks gospel to us in these moments and experi-ences. Androgyny has become one of the most powerful images of our times. It is there in the pretty face of Johnny Depp or the androgynous beauty of Annie Lennox. Gender is a performance we make rather than an assigned and invincible role. Masculinity as well as femininity are in transition. This new situation is at once exciting and terrifying. We might think we are fairly cool about it all. A woman cuts her hair very short. A male student brings his baby into college. But could we stay cool and even cele-brate when a man becomes the woman she has always known herself to be, or if one of the women transgressed the final female taboo and grew a beard? We are as vulnerable and constrained in this part of life as in any other, all of us.

God speaks to us in Christ as we seek to name our gender and to practise it within the context of faith. Some tellings of the doctrine of the Trinity seem determined to put God on the side only of masculinity, and that in its most macho version, mighty and powerful, even unfeeling. What else are we to make of a father who does not suffer? But Jesus gloriously, wonderfully and reassuringly subverts and overturns such an understanding of what it means to be human or divine and offers instead a new, redeemed humanity, in which both male and female are includ-ed, celebrated and affirmed as being bearers of God's being and glory. Jesus fails to be the macho man, but he is the human being. In him there is neither male nor female, or rather there is both and every shade of human grace and style. Even Victorian sentiment reveals what orthodoxy has repressed, that Jesus is not only man, he is also woman, and she is divine.

In thinking about the Trinity, some have suggested that it is the Spirit who is 'she'. But it cannot be right to fix any of the faces of God according to shifting human categories of gender. God can be seen and known in female flesh as well as male, and imaged as mother, friend, lover, just as father. And as each of us struggle to find ourselves or perform our true and redeemed selves on the stage of gender, we may know that God plays every part with as much grace and saving love. In Jesus Christ, all bodies are made new, and all souls find their own name at last.

The female actor Fiona Shaw once famously played Richard II in a controversial production of Shakespeare's play. She writes of her longing for a world in which 'the inconclusion of gender is embraced and accepted, and the imagination can dance elsewhere' (Shaw, in Goodman and de Gay (eds), 1998). In *Twelfth Night*, Shakespeare insists on putting the inconclusion of gender right and everyone goes back to being what they 'ought' to be. I wonder if there is room for a new production in which the characters freely flout the conventions that make gender only a matter of biology or disguise and not a matter of choice. A new production in which swapped gender roles are not simply fodder for comedy or twists of the plot, a new production in which the old markers of male and female are freely and happily transgressed. For there is plenty in the Christian tradition to suggest that gender might be left to its inconclusion, so that the imagination can indeed dance elsewhere. So that, all of us, within the love of God, may be 'all the daughters of our father's or our mother's house and all the brothers and sisters too . . .' Amen.

Conclusion
How to 'preach like a woman'

Throughout this book I have argued that preaching 'like a woman' may be a deliberate choice, a craft developed, a skill honed. It's not either that women will always naturally preach in a certain way or that only the most brave, determined and radical feminists can do it. I believe that any woman can choose and learn to preach in a way that brings her own distinctive voice to the pulpit and to the shaping of the faith. I also think that male preachers might also learn to preach in ways that derive from being more intentionally understanding of their situated experience (rather than assume that their own experience can be straightforwardly universalized as 'human' experience), but that's a book for someone else to write!

In this final chapter I want to draw together some very practical advice for those who would like to 'preach like a woman'. I would recommend that you take some time to explore the world of gender studies. The Church may not always be the best place to start so I suggest you explore the library, bookshop or internet, to find out what people are thinking these days about gender. You might find a course somewhere near you on Women's Studies or something like it and it's often a fascinating and liberating experience to discover how gender looks to those who live outside the boundaries of the Church.

Unless you want to, you don't need to read the latest and most impenetrable feminist philosophy that's available! But you could do things like listen to *Woman's Hour* on Radio 4, look out for films at the nearest arts cinema, and turn to the 'women's' sections in the newspapers. Get a collection of poetry by women. Go to the theatre and the movies and to art galleries looking out for art, for criticism, for protest, for anything at all that women have produced, designed and reflected upon. You will soon get a feel for the ways in which women are living within our culture and for the ways in which our culture is reflecting on women's lives and the question of gender. Follow the leads that appeal to you. Join a women's group of any kind. Learn to enjoy and to draw strength from the company of women. Get to know not only about 'women's issues' but also the real and urgent needs and passions of many women's lives. All of this experience and reflection may become a fruitful place from which to speak on a Sunday and you can take all of this with you into the pulpit.

If you really want to 'preach like a woman' you will be someone who has reflected upon, prayed about, and come to understand and value your own lived experience as a woman both in our culture and in the Church. Your own life experience will be an important resource for your preaching, not as a source of personal anecdotes, but as the ground on which you stand and from which you recognize both the 'otherness' of other's people's lives and also their connections with each other and with you. You will understand that your experience is both particular and unique, but also shaped by the place in which you live, the tradition in which you stand and by the faith you hold and share with others. You will have a degree of self-awareness and an understanding of the impact that your woman's life, body, voice and story have on others as they listen to the gospel from your lips and your body. You will know that in some ways, whether you like it or not, for those who listen, you 'preach like a woman', and you will want to use that consciously for the glory of God and for the good of all those you meet. So learning to preach consciously and deliberately from a woman's life will need time spent in prayer and reflection on the gift and reality of your own embodied life.

It will also be important to wrestle with the history and place of women and women's testimony and experience within the Church. It will be helpful to read some feminist biblical studies and some church history that does more than account for the great men of the past. Study some of the stories of great women saints, from Mary to Mother Theresa and countless women in between. And look carefully at the lives and stories of the women who have frightened the Church by daring to challenge its assumptions and ways, women like those burned as witches in medieval Europe or women like Lavinia Byrne and Sinead O'Connor in our own times, both in their very different ways 'dangerous' for a patriarchal Church. Look for the women of the Bible and the way their stories have been told and retold, forgotten and revived. Find out about extraordinary women of the medieval Church like Julian of Norwich and Hildegard of Bingen. Read the stories of women pioneers like Josephine Butler and Florence Nightingale and find out about the women whose voices have been heard in the Church in our own times, whether calling for the ordination of women, for the feeding of the poor or the care of the dying. But don't make the mistake of thinking that the only women worth reading about or discovering have been famous or notorious. Find out what it's been like for more 'ordinary' women in the Church, from the pillars of the WI to the girls in Magdalene homes, from missionaries and deaconesses to the wives of clergy, from Sunday school teachers to the women who today keep many a local church going. To be interested in women's lives and their significance is definitely not only to be interested in those women who have been exceptional, but it is to take seriously the lives of all women, to give them recognition, dignity and meaning. It is all these voices that must be heard when someone dares to 'preach like a woman'.

But having taken all that as background and commitment, what could it mean to 'preach like a woman', when it comes to the moment of sitting down with a set of Bible readings, and a Sunday service or weekday meeting is looming? And of course, to preach faithfully from within a woman's life doesn't mean that you only preach to or address women! It is to be hoped that whatever words are spoken from the pulpit might bring the light and hope of the gospel to all God's people. In the past preachers have mostly and dominantly been male and there has been an assumption that they can speak for all humanity before God. I do believe that at their most sympathetic, imaginative and inspired, this has been what has happened! But the Church has been impoverished both by living with the assumption that human experience can be generalized, and by hearing so little of the gospel spoken through and from the lives of women. It is one of the great blessings of the Church in our times that more women are speaking the faith, more people of colour, more people with disability, more people who have shared life among those who are poor. My own sense of mission is about empowering women to speak the gospel, to be the theologians, poets and teachers God has called us to be and to seize joyfully the opportunities we are given. But I do not want to replace one falsely generalized humanity with another! When women preach, people see, as sometimes they have not seen before, that voices always come from a particular place, but that such voices can truly speak to all of us. So, Sunday looms and the Bible is open before you . . .

If you want to 'preach like a woman' I suggest the following:

- Read the Bible texts (either those set or those you have chosen) with careful, affectionate attention and with the trust and hope that through your reading, interpreting and speaking, the gospel will be heard. As you read carefully (before turning to any commentaries, sermon internet sites or even conversations with friends), trust your own life experience to provide a context in which the text will unfold.
- Notice any puzzles in the text, any contradictions or anything unexplained. Notice which verses stand out for you or any that you had not noticed in this passage before. If it's a narrative spend some time thinking about the characters. With whom do you identify? Think about the gender of the characters. Ask yourself who is named, who is active or passive, who is the hero or the villain, who is silent and who speaks. If it's an epistle or a piece of legislation or a psalm or any other kind of genre think about its possible origin and imagine how it might have come to be written and why. Who wanted this said so much that it's become part of our Bible? Whose interests does it serve? Is there anyone who would want to challenge it or whose interests are denied in it? Interrogate the text like a detective. But make sure you use your own resources first before you turn to the shelves. Trust your own life to be the place in which the text first has a good hearing.

- Carry the text (or texts) around with you through the week. Take it to the places and people you visit and see what it 'says' there. Make sure that you take it everywhere with you, not just to the library or study, but to the hospital ward and the children's playground, to the supermarket and the cinema, to your women friends and to your family. You could talk about it with people you meet and see what they say. Or just see how your understanding of it changes as you imagine it and remember it in these different places, including the places in which women live and experience their lives. Know that because Bible stories have been so often interpreted in male-dominated and institutionalized contexts, anyone has to work harder to 'read' them outside the library, the academy or the church building.
- Only now turn to the history books and the commentaries to see what you can discover about your text(s). Learn a healthy caution about the books you read and ask to what extent they are interested parties in the search for understanding. Look in the latest and most fashionable commentaries. Look at old and out-of-date ones too, even very ancient ones from the very early days of the Church, since these at least offer you a counter-cultural look at the text. Look at what feminist historians and literary critics have written and see how their comments and discoveries are distinctive. Look for readings of your text from other contexts in the world Church and from lives very different from your own. As well as being cautious about what you read, learn to be cautious about your first thoughts, so that your encounter with text, context, experience and imagination might lead to something creative!
- Find out how your text(s) has been interpreted and used over the centuries in the Church. Is it a text that has set people free, or has it been used to keep people 'in chains'? If it is true that every text bears with it the history of its own interpretation, what history does this text carry? Can you remember any films based on it, any paintings, plays, novels or children's books? What is in your memory about this text? What has it carried to you?

- You will now be ready to make some judgements about your text(s) and to make some decisions about a possible direction for your sermon. Perhaps you have discovered that this text reveals or hides significant things about the place of women within the ancient world (or worlds!) or within the early Church – is there something to draw on here to speak hope for today's world and Church? Perhaps the text reveals real and powerful misogyny that needs to be named and addressed with an openness that is rarely found. Perhaps this text has a powerful history and disturbing history and it is time to change the course of it! Perhaps this text is ready to be taken apart and retold with a different voice.

- Ask how the particular pieces of Scripture with which you are wrestling today relate to the rest of the Bible. What place do they have within it? Are there any texts which they challenge or undo, or are they undone in their turn by others? If the Bible is like a many-voiced conversation, where is the dialogue going at this point? Is there a reply to the scandal or challenge which your text provokes somewhere else in the Bible? Why is this text where it is and what is it trying to do just here? If the conversation continues as the Bible is read and interpreted in the Church what can we say today? What is being said to us, and what, in the light of the whole witness of Scripture, might we want to say in return?

- At this point you need to remember that preaching is about speaking good news! It is not about being clever and inventive for the sake of it, or for making listeners feel guilty or miserable. But it may be that a text that has for centuries been used to speak oppression to many, might, when spoken of in a different voice and from a different place, offer a new moment of redemption. It may also be that a text which has always brought joy and delight to listening congregations will unfold a different joy, or a joy with a new intensity, when preached on from a different voice. Even if you are revealing intense misogyny and abuse, you are revealing it so that it might be condemned and defeated – and that is always good news. Even in telling tragic stories, you are telling them so that the true comedy of the gospel may be heard, so that those crying with pain may come to laugh again.

- In preparing and framing your sermon you need to ask how you are going to convey the good news you have heard from the Bible as it has spoken into your experience and as you have imagined it may do for others. It's never enough just to 'say it' in propositional terms. It's no good simply telling people that this is good news, they have to hear it as good news. It's no good saying that the gospel brings us joy, but people need to see and hear evident joy as you preach. You have to evoke and engage, to take people with you and show them the gospel, not just describe it. So, if you want to convey what a Bible story might mean from a perspective different from the (male) narrator, then tell it again yourself from the point of view of a female character (either already present in the text or one you've imagined). If you want to persuade people that the story is different from another perspective, give them that perspective so that they can see it for themselves. If you want people to understand the force of the scandal of the text, then help them to stand in a place so that they can feel it too. Use invention and imagination, creative retelling and reconstruction to show how differently this text could play out. Don't be afraid to use a new language for a new theology, to embody the new shape you are giving the faith in new styles, languages and forms. If you want to encourage people to imagine God through women's lives, be brave and imaginative in using metaphors and stories that do just that. Don't talk about it with timidity, but do it with bravery and beauty!
- As you prepare your sermon think carefully about those who will hear you. Think of a few selected people who you know might be there and imagine how what you say (or what the text says) will be heard by them. How will those who are poor hear the Beatitudes? How will those who are rich hear the Beatitudes? How will those who are divorced hear Jesus' teaching on marriage? How will those just fallen in love hear what Paul has to say about 'better to marry than to burn'? How will the women in the congregation hear stories in which they only feature as the property of men? How will women hear

the value of their own gender when the gendered metaphors for God are all male? Think carefully about how your own response to the text and the words you say might offer something different, but also how you might be heard. Risk being shocking and saying something new, but act with kindness to your listeners so that they are willing to come with you at least for long enough to understand that you want to bring good news and be faithful to what God is saying. It's worth being unpopular for good causes, but not for being thoughtless in the way you've expressed something! Remember that on any Sunday all kinds of people may be listening and may be bearing all sorts of tender wounds. You needn't worry about being too radical (you're never going to be as radical as Jesus himself!), though you might want to think carefully about how your being radical will be heard and felt by your listeners. There will be some of them (believe me, in any congregation you can name!) who will be overcome with relief that at last someone is speaking something directly from and to their experience or the experience of those they love. There will be those for whom the 'decent' theology of the Church they have known leaves so much unsaid and denied. For some there may be incomprehension or resistance, and for them you will need to signal that you are speaking with the integrity of a rooted faith and that your desire is that God's good news should be heard. You may be conducting a kind of 'ministry in exile', but you will always be speaking to those who have known exile themselves (for a whole variety of human reasons) and who long with you to find a way home.

- Believe that you are called to preach to all God's people, and that God has given you a life and a faith from which to speak. But don't take yourself too seriously either. Gentle, kindly humour and laughter connect us with other people and reveal that joy is always ready to break through. They also reassure others that we are together in this experience of discovering what it means to be human before God. The best kind of humour for a preacher is not necessarily the kind that tells jokes or that has them rolling in the aisles, but the kind that is about recognition, about naming the kind of absurd truth

185

that makes the gospel truly comic. The best kind of humour topples the powerful, but also raises up the humble. God's revolutionary gospel is more like the carnival of clowns than the raised fists of angry rebels. It used to be thought by many that women are not so good at humour, but we have learned that when the most radical and holy changes come they are accompanied by laughter and dancing. This too is part of what it means to 'preach like a woman'.

A women's group might be a great place to begin to find your own voice as a preacher. Find a space where you can feel safe enough to do what some might think 'indecent' theology. But don't stay there. Because the Church needs to hear the gospel through our lives and from our lips. The Church needs those who will speak with power and passion of the gospel of God's love for all people and for all creation. A kind of silence falls when our voices are denied. So, let the silence be broken and let it be said many times in our churches that she preached 'like a woman'.

Bibliography

Alexander, L., 'Sisters in Adversity: Retelling Martha's Story', in Brooke, G. J. (ed.), *Women in the Biblical Tradition*. Edwin Mellen Press, New York, 1992, pp. 167–86.

Althaus-Reid, M., *From Feminist Theology to Indecent Theology*. SCM Press, London, 2004.

Althaus-Reid, M., *Indecent Theology: Theological Perversions in Sex, Gender and Politics*. Routledge, London, 2000.

Beckford, R., *Jesus is Dread: Black Theology and Black Culture in Britain*. Darton, Longman and Todd, London, 1998.

Berger, J., *To the Wedding*. Bloomsbury, London, 1995.

Berger, J., *Ways of Seeing*. BBC, London, 1972.

Brown Taylor, B., 'The Weekly Wrestling Match', in Graves, M. (ed.), *What's the Matter with Preaching Today?* Westminster John Knox Press, London, 2004, pp. 171–82.

Brueggemann, W., *Inscribing the Text*. Augsburg Fortress, Minneapolis, 2004.

Buechner, F., *The Sacred Journey: A Memoir of Early Days*. Harper-SanFrancisco, New York, 1982.

Burghardt, W. J., *Preaching: The Art and the Craft*. Paulist Press, New York, 1987.

Buttrick, D., 'A Fearful Pulpit, a Wayward Land', in Graves, M. (ed.), *What's the Matter with Preaching Today?* Westminster John Knox Press, London, 2004, pp. 37–50.

Carter Florence, A., 'Put Away Your Sword! Taking the Torture out of the Sermon', in Graves, M. (ed.), *What's the Matter with Preaching Today?* Westminster John Knox Press, London, 2004, pp. 93–108.

Cotes, M., 'Women, Silence and Fear (Mark 16:8)', in Brooke, G. J. (ed.), *Women in the Biblical Tradition*. Edwin Mellen Press, New York, 1992, pp. 150–66.

cummings, e. e., *selected poems 1923–1958*. Faber and Faber, London, 1969.

Dalrymple, W., *From the Holy Mountain*. Flamingo, London, 1998.

Day, D., Astley, J. and Francis, L. J. (eds), *A Reader on Preaching: Making Connections*. Ashgate, Aldershot, 2005.

Derrida, J., 'Cogito and the History of Madness', in *Writing and Difference*, translated with an Introduction and Additional Notes by Alan Bass. University of Chicago Press, Chicago, 1978, pp. 31–63.

Durber, S., 'The Female Reader of the Parables of the Lost', *Journal for the Study of the New Testament* 45, 1992, pp. 59–78.

Durber, S. and Walton, H. (eds), *Silence in Heaven: A Book of Women's Preaching*, SCM Press, London, 1994.

Eadie, D., *Grain in Winter*. Epworth, Peterborough, 1999.

Emerson Fosdick, H., 'What is the Matter with Preaching?' reprinted in Graves, M. (ed.), *What's the Matter with Preaching Today?* Westminster John Knox Press, London, 2004, pp. 7–19.

Goodman, L. and de Gay, J. (eds), *The Routledge Reader in Gender and Performance*. Routledge, London, 1998.

Hopkins, G. Manley, *A Selection of his Poems and Prose*. Penguin, London, 1958.

Jasper, D., 'On Systematizing the Unsystematic. A Response', in Marsh, C. and Ortiz, G. (eds), *Explorations in Theology and Film*. Blackwell, Oxford, 1997, pp. 235–44.

Jennings, E., *Praises*. Carcanet, Manchester, 1998.

Kaye, E., Lees, J. and Thorpe, K., *Daughters of Dissent*. URC, London, 2004.

Keenan, B., *An Evil Cradling*. Vintage, London, 1993.

Long, T., 'No News is Bad News', in Graves, M. (ed.), *What's the Matter with Preaching Today?* Westminster John Knox Press, London, 2004, pp. 145–7.

Moltmann-Wendel, E., *The Women Around Jesus*. Crossroad, New York, 1990.

Moore, S., *Poststructuralism and the New Testament*. Fortress Press, Minneapolis, 1994.

Ostriker, A. Suskin, *Feminist Revision and the Bible*. Blackwell, Oxford, 1993.

Pearson, A., *I Don't Know How She Does It*. Chatto and Windus, London, 2002.

Pearson Mitchell, E. (ed.), *Those Preachin' Women: Sermons by Black Women Preachers*. Judson Press, Valley Forge, 1985.

Purvis-Smith, V., 'Gender and the Aesthetic of Preaching', in Day, D., Astley J. and Francis, L. J. (eds), *A Reader on Preaching: Making Connections*. Ashgate, Aldershot, 2005, pp. 224–9.

Radford Ruether, R., *Sexism and God-Talk*. SCM Press, London, 1983.

Rees, C. (ed.), *Voices of this Calling*. Canterbury Press, Norwich, 2002.

Schüssler Fiorenza, E., *In Memory of Her: A Feminist Theological Construction of Christian Origins*. SCM Press, London, 1983.

Slee, N., *Praying like a Woman*. SPCK, London, 2004.

Trible, P., *Texts of Terror: Literary Feminist Readings of Biblical Narratives*. SCM Press, London, 1984.

Troeger, T. H., *The Parable of Ten Preachers*. Abingdon, Nashville, 1992.

Troeger, T. H., 'Emerging New Standards in the Evaluation of Effective Preaching', in Day, D., Astley J. and Francis, L. J. (eds), *A Reader on Preaching: Making Connections*. Ashgate, Aldershot, 2005, pp. 116–26.

Van Wolde, E., *Stories of the Beginning: Genesis 1–11 and Other Creation Stories*. SCM Press, London, 1996.

Walton, H., 'Breaking Open the Bible', in Graham, E., and Halsey, M. (eds), *Life Cycles: Women and Pastoral Care*. SPCK, London, 1993.

Williams, D. S., *Sisters in the Wilderness: The Challenge of Womanist God-Talk*. Orbis Books, New York, 2002.

Willimon, W. H., *Proclamation and Theology*. Abingdon Press, Nashville, 2005.

Index of biblical references